I0065625

Endorsements

I n the more than 30 years I've known Gary Mottershead as both a client and associate coach for Strategic Coach®, I've observed his rare ability to adapt to new circumstances, gain lessons from his unique experiences, use those lessons to achieve tremendous success, and transmit his wisdom to Strategic Coach®'s entrepreneurial clients to help them grow and navigate through an ever-changing world. With *Nimble Future*, Gary consolidates his insights into a clear and simple guide that encourages the reader to think about their thinking, prepares them for what's coming over the next two decades in terms of technology and new complexities, and provides the keys to future-proofing their business and overcoming fears and obstacles. A must-read for the future-focused, always-growing entrepreneur.

—*Dan Sullivan*
Co-Founder & President, Strategic Coach®

I'm proud to endorse Gary's latest book, *Nimble Future*. I've known Gary for over 30 years, and he has been my coach at Strategic Coach® for more than ten years. In this book, he brings his wisdom, insights, and stories together so that we can all navigate a nimble future.

When I led the first team to sail the Northwest Passage, we chose a boat that was the ultimate in nimbleness to sail fast, haul across the ice, get off the stormy ocean, and allowed us not just to survive but to succeed in one of toughest environments in the world.

Gary is an amazing coach and communicator because he understands how to ask the right questions, how to challenge you to be nimble, how to think deeper, and what makes your future better.

A nimble mindset is so important as we navigate an unknowable future. All we know is that the future will not be like the past. Read this book to gain a deeper understanding for creating your own nimble future.

—Jeff MacInnis
Explorer and Entrepreneur, First Person to Sail the 4,000km Northwest Passage
Author of the best-selling book Polar Passage
Founder and President at WIN Thinking

Having known Gary on a personal level for years, I wholeheartedly endorse his latest masterpiece, *Nimble Future: Reinvent Your Past, Protect Your Present, Engage in Your Future*. Gary, an exemplary entrepreneur and visionary, distills decades of experience into this insightful guide.

In *Nimble Future*, he not only imparts invaluable business strategies but shares authentic wisdom gained through facing challenges head-on. Gary's commitment to building robust relationships, emphasizing clarity of purpose, and demystifying technology resonates profoundly.

This book stands out not just for its profound insights but for Gary's genuine desire to help others. If you're searching for a mentor within the pages of a book, "Nimble Future" is the personal guide you've been looking for.

—Ted Kerr
CFP®, Founder/CEO of Touchstone Capital, Inc.
Author of Killing Time, A Parable for the Present Age

Gary has the rare capability of being firmly grounded in a strong foundation yet agile enough to adapt for the future. If you're looking for insights that stand the test of time while continuing to grow, this book is for you.

—Evan Ryan
Founder of Teammate AI
Author of AI as Your Teammate

Gary Mottershead has a great talent at cutting through the noise and getting to the root of issues. I always appreciate his insights and his deep thoughtfulness. *Nimble Future* will help sharpen your thinking of what really matters in our future. Sharpening your thinking will create clearer options, and that will generate confidence in how best to face whatever the future holds.

—Daniel Hammond
Business Interrogation LLC / Customer Driven Leadership LLC.
Author of Customer Driven Leadership,
The Disciplined CEO, *and* Success Secrets Of Disruptors

Nimble Future is about achieving your desires and appreciating what you achieve. It is filled with practical wisdom and tools to help you make sense of your unique journey through your past, present, and future.

As we are confronted with the exponential growth of technology, data, and change itself, Gary reminds us to relax because technology never takes hold faster than the rate at which people are ready to use it.

Another key takeaway from the book is to focus on what doesn't change rather than what will. It is important to recognize the difference between timely strategies, which relate to what you are doing or pursuing now . . . and timeless strategies, which relate to what you have done, what you are doing, and what you will do. It is the timeless strategies that shape who you are and who you are becoming.

—Howard Getson
CEO, Capitalogix

NIMBLE
FUTURE

Reinterpret Your Past,
Protect Your Present,
Engage in Your Future

N I M B L E
FUTURE

Reinterpret Your Past,
Protect Your Present,
Engage in Your Future

GARY MOTTERSHEAD

ethos
collective

NIMBLE FUTURE © 2024 by Gary Mottershead. All rights reserved.

Printed in the United States of America

Published by Ethos Collective™
PO Box 43, Powell, OH 43065
www.ethoscollective.vip

This book contains material protected under international and federal copyright laws and treaties. Any unauthorized reprint or use of this material is prohibited. No part of this book may be reproduced or transmitted in any form or by any means, electronic or mechanical, including photocopying, recording, or by any information storage and retrieval system, without express written permission from the author.

LCCN: 2023923687
Paperback ISBN: 978-1-63680-247-3
Hardcover ISBN: 978-1-63680-248-0
e-book ISBN: 978-1-63680-249-7

Available in paperback, hardcover, and e-book.

Any Internet addresses (websites, blogs, etc.) and telephone numbers printed in this book are offered as a resource. They are not intended in any way to be or imply an endorsement by Ethos Collective™, nor does Ethos Collective™ vouch for the content of these sites and numbers for the life of this book.

Some names and identifying details have been changed to protect the privacy of individuals.

Nimble Future is dedicated to my wife, Karen, who has encouraged me to engage in our future for more than 45 years.

Contents

Foreword

G ary Mottershead has a gift. I've seen him do it time and time again. He can look into the future with clarity and courage and then readjust to engage that new reality, creating a bigger impact for everyone involved. Thankfully, he's put a framework behind this genius, and we're all better because of it.

Welcome to *Nimble Future*.

Our relationship with time is both intricate and profound. We march through life, facing change at every turn, but when we look back, our path is almost unrecognizable. Especially in the world of business, where uncertainty looms like a shadow, we find ourselves at a crossroads.

Will we forge ahead in faith or let fear bind us to the past?

Gary's insightful book invites us to reexamine the time we have and even reinvest it with agility and purpose. Drawing from psychology, philosophy, and practical wisdom, Gary explains not only how to navigate change, but how to adapt so that change becomes the key to your success rather than its inhibitor.

Gary highlights so many important guiding principles, and he does so with the conviction of someone experienced in managing the twists and turns of life. He tells us that a crystal-clear purpose is the North Star of a successful business. Purpose illuminates the darkest corners of uncertainty, and once you can see clearly in the light of that purpose, the game changes.

Fear paralyzes. Facts empower.

Gary shows us how to shift from fear-driven reactions to evidence-based decisions. In doing so, we unlock the door to success, even in the face of adversity. Further, we see that adversity, especially when it does lead to failure, need not be fatal. Instead, it becomes a stepping stone to innovation. Gary's insights reveal how setbacks can fertilize the soil of creativity, yielding unexpected blooms.

Gary can also personally testify to the idea that long-term relationships are the currency of business. He emphasizes the value of genuine connections—those that withstand storms and celebrate victories. He shows us how our belief system is the bedrock of resilience then he teaches us how to protect and nurture this inner asset.

As you embark on this transformative journey through *Nimble Future*, remember that success isn't merely about profit margins or market share. It's about the legacy we leave, the lives we touch, and the impact we make. Whether you're a seasoned entrepreneur or a budding visionary, these pages hold the keys to unlock your potential.

Embrace the uncertainty. Let faith be your compass. And may your business thrive, not despite the challenges, but because of them.

—Dr. Kary Oberbrunner
CEO, *Wall Street Journal* and *USA Today*
Bestselling Author of 13 books

Note to Reader

Dear Reader,

Thank you for choosing to read *Nimble Future: Reinvent Your Past, Protect Your Present, Engage in Your Future.*

This book was written to help you navigate the fast-paced world we live in and empower you to set the direction for your life that is grounded in your experience and determined by your vision of your future.

The book is based on my life experiences as a husband, father, and grandfather, as well as 30+ years as an entrepreneur and 25+ years as a coach to more than 3000 entrepreneurs.

This journey began in January 2020. My company, GCP Industrial Products, was then 20 years old, and the idea of 20/20 vision got stuck in my head. I asked myself, "What if we could use our past experiences to help set us up for the future, the next 20 years?!"

The writing began one chapter at a time. The working title was *Hindsight to Foresight: Future Proofing Your Business.* For those of you who remember what happened to the world in March 2020, the COVID-19 pandemic hit the entire world, an event not seen in more than 100 years.

By March, half the book was written, and I continued to finish the second half by mid-2020. The world, my world, was significantly different at the end of the book than it was at the beginning.

Faced with the unprecedented challenges in both our business and personal lives, work on the book stopped for more than two years. It was not until my wife, Karen, and I finally got our 40th wedding anniversary trip two and half years later that I reread the book on the beach in Barbados.

I felt that if the message of the book could not be relevant after what we all experienced, then it did not deserve to be published. However, to my surprise and delight, the premise and message of what is now titled *Nimble Future: Reinvent your Past, Protect your Present, Engage in your Future* held more relevance in the post-COVID world than it did before.

The book is a quick read. You can read it all at one time or just a chapter or two. Each chapter stands on its own and is designed to help you think about situations you are facing, how to make sense of them for you, and, most importantly, how to move forward.

I believe we all need to have filters, ways, or criteria to screen out the data and information that bombards us every day. Most of it is not useful for effectively living our lives. It is distracting, confusing, and a waste of time. So, how do we ignore it? How do we determine what's important and not important? This is what the book is all about—helping you sort the "wheat from the chaff," using an agricultural term.

Wishing you all the best as you engage in your future!

Sincerely,

Gary Mottershead

Introduction

I started to write this book in January 2020, when the first indications of something called COVID-19 were circulating in China. My company, GCP Industrial Products (GCP), was just over twenty years old then. We had built a successful business entity, primarily with Chinese manufacturing partners and American customers. My first book, *Guanxi: The China You Never Read About*, looked back on how it all came to be.

But I'm primarily a futurist. So, my idea for this book, *Nimble Future*, was to take what I had learned over the past two decades and talk about what I see happening over the next twenty years.

When I started my first business in 1989 called Recovery Technologies, I knew literally nothing about being an entrepreneur. My first eight years provided me with only a small portion of the experience I needed to become successful. When I started GCP in 1999, many difficult lessons lay ahead for me and my team. But I had a vision, and I didn't give up, mostly because I truly believed we were building something with a higher purpose. We were one of the first companies in the world to focus on utilizing recycled tire rubber for our products. And in China, we helped turn domestic factories into world-class producers.

Shortly after I completed the first few chapters of this book, the world was hit by the first wave of COVID lockdowns. That changed everything for me personally, for my company, for the country in which I live (Canada), and for the world. However, it did *not* change the way I viewed the future, nor did it change the value of this book. What I intended to say from the beginning remains true today.

As my mentor Dan Sullivan, the co-founder of Strategic Coach®, says: "The problem is not the problem. It's how to think about the problem that is the problem."

If we don't know how to think about the challenges we'll face as we move forward into the next twenty years, then we have a problem. This book was written to help you think about what's coming in the next two decades and how to be ready for it.

CHAPTER ONE

What Doesn't Change Matters

I very frequently get the question: "What's going to change in the next ten years?" And that is a very interesting question; it's a very common one. I almost never get the question: "What's not going to change in the next ten years?" And I submit to you that that second question is actually the more important of the two—because you can build a business strategy around the things that are stable in time.

—Jeff Bezos, Founder of Amazon

Artificial intelligence. Self-driving cars. ChatGPT. Machine learning. Information overload. The pandemic. Today's business world can appear to be a rapidly changing, scary place.

But it doesn't have to be.

The idea of change can appear fearsome only because we tend to see it as something we can't necessarily control. But when we recognize it for what it is—a constant—we're able to form adaptation strategies and have future planning discussions, where the concept of change becomes a factor under our control. Any fears associated with change and the rate of change are negated, and change now works *for* us rather than against us.

In fact, the best strategy to "future-proof" your personal and professional life for the next twenty years is to focus on aspects of the business that will not change rather than the ones that will.

I like to use a sailing metaphor when making the point that change is a malleable factor. Imagine change as wind. When sailors anticipate a gust of wind, they position their sails in order to use the wind to their benefit rather than fighting its resistance. Sailors will always tell you that while they can't change the winds, they can certainly adjust the position of their sails to make the wind work for them.

Jeff Bezos sees it the same way. From his perspective, Amazon customers have long been clear about exactly what they want; unsurprisingly, they want low prices and fast delivery times. He notes that no matter how much everything else changes over the next decade, Amazon customers will never come to him and ask for higher prices and slower delivery times. Bezos approaches the future with these two basic rudiments as his foundation.

When you plan for the future, focus first and foremost on the core strengths of your business.

As I reflect on my own business and look forward to the next twenty years, I know one thing for sure about GCP: our customers will always need products. That will never change. We also deliver the best products in our industry, so by extension, our customers will always need *our* products. Like good sailors, we set the sails of our business to accommodate that central fact and create strategies that enable us to thrive, no matter how strongly or in which direction the winds of change blow.

Our creative license is stifled when we feel overwhelmed by change. But, adopting this type of mindset when considering the future of your business allows for a clear new focus on creativity and the potential to achieve objectives on higher levels.

With this in mind, I'd like to outline what I see as four keys to "future-proofing" your business:

1. *Building Strong Relationships:* As entrepreneurs and business leaders, we often think we have to worry about every single little detail of our operations. We don't. Our attention should be heavily focused on relationships—those we have with our customers, suppliers, family, and colleagues.

2. *Clarity of Purpose:* Clarifying purpose and communicating it effectively so that all stakeholders know what's expected of them is absolutely critical.

3. *Purpose of Technology:* Technology does serve a useful purpose. But it's important that we understand it for what it is, and we don't allow it to overwhelm us.

4. *Moderating Information:* Develop filters to extract only requisite information to avoid information overload.

The Importance of Relationships

I can get together with my high school friends today and still feel as close to them as I did in our teenage years. Strong relationships stand the test of time when we put in the work to cultivate them. The same can be true in business.

Being aware of the dangers facing your customers and your business segment in general is important. But seeing the opportunity to derive strength from them is critical.

Allow me to give you an example.

In the mid-2000s, GCP experienced our first major business hurdle. This was mostly because I personally lost sight of what was important. We were in serious trouble.

Unbeknownst to us, one of our main business partners in China began dealing with other companies without notifying us because they believed we were failing them. So, I gambled with an all-or-nothing strategy; I traveled to China to make an impassioned pitch on behalf of the business in an attempt to salvage our relationship.

I spoke honestly, and I genuinely communicated my perceived importance of our business relationship and my sincere hopes that we could retrieve the bond we once had. When I was finished, my business partner looked me in the eye and said:

"Gary, if you believe in yourself, we believe in you."

My demonstration of sincerity had made the difference. The strong relationships I had built over the years of doing business in China saved my company when I led it into difficulties. This is why I believe developing strong relationships and consistently cultivating those relationships should be your first objective in future-proofing your business.

———◈———

At GCP, we believe it's important to have what I call "customer intimacy." For example, we have a client in Louisville, Kentucky, who, until recently, had been filling out all his order forms by hand. A member of my staff showed him how to use a spreadsheet so that he could save time and do it more efficiently.

These are intangible aspects of a relationship that reinforce the strength of their foundations. This is truly how you achieve success on a larger scale—the relationships we develop serve as the foundation, and we build upon it by making it easier, cheaper, and faster to do business with us.

In order to succeed in the development and cultivation of fundamentally solid relationships, you have to surround yourself with like-minded people who share the same values and behaviours. Trust, loyalty, and positivity are personality traits that can't be taught, but they make all the difference in the world when it comes to building genuine relationships that last.

Confidence is also a critical behaviour in forging strong relationships. Associating with people who complement not only your strengths but also your weaknesses is key—almost as important as the ability to identify your own weaknesses, recognizing that aligning with colleagues who make up those gaps makes the enterprise that much stronger and more successful. The smartest people always seek to surround themselves with those smarter than they are, regardless of your business segment or your station in life.

The Need For Clarity of Purpose

The second key learning I'd like to pass on to you is the need to have clarity of purpose and clearly communicate it.

Here's a famous example. The United States Army takes great pains to make sure every soldier knows the overall mission objective, as well as his or her individual role in the mission and what specific responsibilities they're required to carry out during the mission. This way, should the execution of the mission be compromised in any way, everyone still knows what needs to be done.

The approach used by the Russian Army is quite different. They choose to implement a centralization strategy, in which neither frontline soldiers nor their leaders know the overall battle plan. If something goes awry, they have to pause and relay situational information back to Moscow, then await new orders. This is a recipe for disaster.

Successful business execution models more closely resemble the former example above. Without clarity of purpose and an effective communication strategy to ensure a common understanding among everyone involved, stakeholder confusion and uncertainty can give way to paralysis, leaving your business unable to execute successfully.

The Purpose of Technology

My third key learning is that recent technological advancements we tend to hear about all the time are *not* going to rise up and come crashing down on us, destroying our businesses. History proves this.

Over my lifetime, the way we transmit and receive information has changed significantly. Think bulky black-and-white television with antennae and channel knobs versus wafer-thin LED 4K smart TVs with plasma screens that seemingly float against the wall, streaming high-definition, breathtakingly sharp images. Or wall-mounted party-line telephones with those big, long, curly cords giving way to the smartphone—a miniature computer we carry around in our pockets capable of completing thousands of tasks.

Those are just two examples. But neither of them arrived overnight.

The first mobile phones appeared after car phones provided users the luxury of making and receiving calls from their automobiles. An upstart company called BlackBerry®, founded by two university roommates, was a pager company before its meteoric rise and absolute domination of the handheld device market. During this period, none of us could have imagined BlackBerry was anything less than invincible. But in 2005, Apple® released the first iteration of the iPhone®, nearly putting BlackBerry out of business and significantly changing the cellular phone landscape again.

Why did the iPhone succeed over its heretofore dominant pre-decessor? Because it was easier to use and offered more features. The iPhone's user interface was the main reason for its success, not the technology.

Technology can leave our mouths agape with dazzling features, but until someone makes it easy for us to work with new technology, we never take advantage of it. That's simply the way our relationship with technology is always going to be.

The same will be true of self-driving cars, artificial intelligence, and robotics. And what about 3D printing? It's actually been around for forty years, but it's just finding its way into mainstream use. Why?

Because technology never takes hold faster than the rate at which people are ready to use it.

This is why I believe the third point in future-proofing your business is to keep in mind that technology—commonly perceived as the means by which AI will rise up and effectively wipe out humanity—can and should serve a useful purpose, as dictated by us humans.

Moderating Information Overload

We can dictate the means through which we use technology, but no human is equipped to handle the massive flow of information that is deluging us each day. Information filtering is a requirement to avoid becoming overwhelmed and drowning in an ocean of information.

The filtering system I developed for myself involves the creation of what I call *The Information Hierarchy.*

The lowest level of the Hierarchy is *raw data.* The reality is that most people won't see the value in raw data because it's just a bunch of numbers.

The next level is *information.* We tend to regard Information as being a bit more valuable than simple raw data, but people don't start to truly value it until it becomes *knowledge.*

When you've taken the information and developed it into a context that people can use to make decisions, that's knowledge.

The fourth level is called *wisdom.* By now, you've been able to distill that data, that information, that knowledge, and morph it into something more expansive and significant—something of greater permanence that develops into more of a mindset and a way of being. Businesspeople and entrepreneurs have done this for ages.

Don't be intimidated by the ever-increasing volumes of information coming at you in today's rapidly changing world. Assess the information at a pace comfortable to you, filter it based on what you think is essential, and translate it in a way that's meaningful. I've always believed that it's really important that if you possess the information, it's your responsibility to communicate it in such a way that other people can possess it too, not just hear you verbalize the information, but really and truly *get* it, and own it.

When you can assess, filter, and synthesize pools of information into personal wisdom that can be used towards achieving your goals, future-proofing your business will seem elementary.

Purpose & Passion

These concepts will serve as common themes throughout the remaining chapters of this book, in tandem with the notion I've always believed to be absolutely critical to business success in any capacity: you must have a purpose and a passion for what you do.

Simon Sinek gave a TED talk in 2009 called *Start with Why*[1], where he describes the three concentric circles of business: What, How, and Why. Your why is in the center—it's the very core of your business. When people initially buy, they're buying your why. If they don't buy your why first, you may as well forget about it.

Back to Apple again for a moment. Apple boasted impressive next-level technology, but they made it easy for us to use. That was the attraction; that was the why that initially compelled people to buy Apple products.

Yes, it may sound cliché. But it goes without saying that if you want to be successful, you have to have passion. You have to have that fire. This isn't something you can fake or marginalize. It's at the very core of everything you do.

People pick up on that passion. They're moved by that passion. Passion is the factor that can make the difference between succeeding and failing in any pursuit. The mountains get moved only when you're able to channel your passion, and you put yourself in a position to define your own brand of change.

A classic example is the U.S. moon landing mission of the 1960s. President John F. Kennedy told Americans that the U.S.A. would put a man on the moon by the end of the decade. At that time, the United States was lagging behind the Soviet Union in what was called the "space race."

Did JFK or anyone at NASA have any idea how to put a man on the moon? None whatsoever. But everybody involved had a burning passion to make it happen. There was a palpable excitement. Everyone had a singular focus, everyone was driven, and they made it happen. It happened not because anyone knew how it would happen, but by believing that they had the ability to indeed *make* it happen and that it would, *in fact,* happen, they worked towards their goal and were able to achieve it.

Since the day I saw Neil Armstrong take those first steps on the moon, I've believed that if you really have that passion and will to make something happen, you can do it. And where others are concerned, passion is contagious. After you clearly communicate exactly what needs to be done, your passion will take care of the rest.

Business is no different. We see a lot of entrepreneurial success stories: Jeff Bezos, Richard Branson, Arianna Huffington, Steve Jobs, and Oprah Winfrey, to name a few. Oftentimes, we only witness the grandiosity of their successes, the vast measures of their achievements. But there were also struggles. It's important to know there were hardships along the way—dark, uncertain periods that likely compelled them to consider just giving up, maybe more than once.

However, these people and other successful entrepreneurs have overcome these difficulties for two reasons.

One, they had a clear vision of what they wanted to accomplish and continued to work toward it, regardless of how difficult it may have seemed or how many times others told them it wasn't possible.

The second reason we can attribute to their success is their willingness to make a firm commitment. Not just a simple, obligatory commitment. I'm talking about the kind of commitment that means killing everything else off, leaving themselves no other option but the way forward. That's a clearly defined purpose, and that's exemplary passion.

On a personal note, I believe it's important to always set a new goal before achieving the last one. In my late fifties, I decided I wanted to be in better shape at sixty-five than I was at that time. It took a lot of effort, but I did it. Now, I've decided I want to be in better shape when I turn seventy than I was at sixty-five. And I'm going to do it.

When I commit to do something, I do everything in my power to make it happen. It's a personal axiom as true in my business life as it is in my personal life.

I feel like it's a talent I have. Why would I not want to utilize that God-given talent to make the world a better place? To make a difference? To help people grow and truly *thrive?* I've always believed we're put on this planet for a reason. There's an apt quote for this sentiment I believe can be attributed to Bill Gates:

"With wealth comes responsibility. With great wealth comes greater responsibility."

I felt that way long before I heard that expression. I've always been a pretty smart guy who could figure things out. I knew if I wanted to be a useful and valuable part of this world, I needed to put the talents that God gave me to the best possible use.

Making money is a convenient by-product of applying these talents. But what other achievements am I capable of when I maximize these talents? How could I make a real difference? It took a long time for me to figure out the answer to that question.

The following chapters will examine my journey towards arriving at that answer.

CHAPTER TWO

The Future Impacts of Technology

Technology is a useful servant but a dangerous master.
—Historian Christian Lous Lange, Nobel Peace
Prize winner

I n business, technology can be a friend or foe.

Consider the sweeping advances in technology that have happened over the last twenty years and what's expected to happen over the next twenty. The changes resulting from these advances that we've already seen have disrupted businesses in many ways. As such, the changes still to come are bound to disrupt your business - unless you learn how to position your business ahead of these changes and adapt to them. If you're able to do that, then you can turn the tables - and you and your business become the disruptor in your field, not the disrupted.

Look at what Uber® has done to the taxi business. Or what Zoom has done to the video conferencing business. Neither one was an overnight success. But when the public was ready for their products, the two brands became ubiquitous in their respective industries.

I sincerely believe that most technological change over the past twenty years has had a positive impact on people, society, and business, despite some natural human resistance. And I think that trend will continue over the next twenty years. Technology will, on balance, improve our lives.

Consequently, businesses have to adapt. Technological change is inevitable, and history tells us that standing still in the face of it all but guarantees that you and your business will be left behind.

The good news is that we have a choice in terms of how we interact with technological innovation and how we adapt to it. The main objective in making this choice is an assurance that technology is our servant, not our master.

In order to become the disruptor, we need to harness technological advancements, effectively manage the change the advancements initiate, and use this change to our advantage. Deciding whether you're able to use technology to your advantage in a given circumstance requires saying "yes" to one of three questions:

1. *Does the technology solve your problem?*

2. *Does it create an opportunity?*

3. *Does it complement the strengths you already have?*

To answer such questions, it may be helpful to go back and examine the last twenty years to access examples of some of the more significant technological changes that have affected businesses and entrepreneurs over that period and determine what we can learn from them.

The last two decades have witnessed the phenomenal growth of the Internet, as well as vast improvements in communications, banking, and transportation. The companies that have adapted well to these changes are successful. The companies that have not—think Kodak—crumbled in the wake of technological evolution.

Kodak was founded in 1888 and had become so dominant in the photography sector that by 1976, eighty-five percent of all film cameras and ninety percent of all film sold in the United States could be attributed to the company. During this same period, an engineer at Kodak invented the world's first digital camera. When the engineer presented his invention to Kodak executives, they were unimpressed, wondering why anyone would want to look at photos on their television sets instead of in print format.

The groundbreaking invention was largely dismissed, and Kodak filed for bankruptcy in 2012. As powerful and dominant as some of these corporations seemed, failing to recognize the need to evolve and adapt alongside the advent of technology has proven disastrous.

The growth and ubiquity of the Internet began shortly after we founded GCP. We benefited because the Internet allowed us to build a complete back shop with only a few people and without having to make huge investments in infrastructure. We could communicate faster, easier, and better. And we can say the same for most small-to-medium-sized businesses.

At GCP, we evaluated the advantages of using new technological advancements to reduce operational costs. This led us to use

VOIP (Voice Over Internet Protocol) in favour of an expensive telephony system from a large network provider, and VOIP now governs all of our communications. It's a great example of how the Internet, and more generally technology, has revolutionized the scale of business opportunity.

Another incredible Internet advancement has been online banking. At GCP, we've been doing all our banking with our Chinese suppliers online for the past five to ten years. Previously, we had used letters of credit, but they were clumsy and required a lot of paperwork. Banking online also minimizes exposure to fraud.

Curiously, it's much more difficult to conduct similar transactions online with our American customers. The United States doesn't have the seamless banking system we enjoy here in Canada. For example, receiving wire transfers from our American customers can be very challenging. For this reason, one of our longest-standing customers still writes us cheques by hand for $100,000 to $300,000 and sends them to us by courier every Thursday. In this sense, being adaptable cuts both ways. When a valued customer insists on doing things in a way they're comfortable with, we have to concede and adapt to their preferences.

Advancements in technology have also led to improvements in the way we travel. Modern aircraft have been engineered to fly further, making it possible for me to fly directly to China to meet with my business partners at my convenience. Peripheral aspects of air travel have become more efficient as well, making the entire span of a single trip so much easier, right from booking flights online through customs and immigration checks and the amenities afforded passengers on the flight itself. And with the advent of technology that will allow for procedures like facial recognition, efficiency improves again, as does our enjoyment of the overall experience.

So, what's next? Over the next twenty years, I see a few major trends that will fundamentally change how we conduct business: data management using artificial intelligence, self-driving cars, blockchain, and our evolving use of social media channels.

Artificial Intelligence

From an AI standpoint, the ability to gather and synthesize data for strategic purposes offers a tremendous business advantage. For example, at GCP, we're creating predictive data analysis models that anticipate what a customer is going to order.

Currently, when the customer makes an order, we contact the production facility, the factory fulfils the order, and they ship it either to us or directly to the customer. This process is slow and entirely reactive and can take up to six months.

Using data in a more expedient manner will enable us to optimize processes in terms of speed and efficiency, benefiting everyone involved. My goal is to use data we've already accumulated and incorporate artificial intelligence to achieve a "seventy-thirty" supply objective—shipping seventy percent of the product ordered to customers within thirty days of the customer placing the order. Accomplishing this objective would realize some significant benefits, most importantly, our customers experiencing less downtime, which in turn results in better returns for my suppliers. Achieving

The 70-30 Supply Solution™ would result in a win-win-win situation.

Autonomous Vehicles

One of the biggest changes I anticipate in the next twenty years will be the prevalence of autonomous vehicles. This may sound strange given the volume of negative publicity surrounding them recently, but there are a lot of fundamental reasons to justify the inevitability of self-driving cars.

First, Uber and similar companies badly want self-driving cars, given driver remuneration comprises half of their annual operating costs. Similarly, companies producing self-driving cars see a massive market developing for their product.

My son and I were discussing this topic the other day, and he commented that twenty years from now, it will seem odd that people were actually encouraged to drive cars, given accident and fatality rates. A friend mentioned to me recently that he lost his uncle in a car crash caused by a drunk driver, saying that if we had self-driving cars, his uncle would be alive today. The technology is progressively developing, and current bugs will eventually be worked out, making autonomous vehicles the safest way to travel.

Not surprisingly, the main companies currently building and developing them—Cruise, Aurora, and Argo AI—are all technology companies. These companies collect data on every trip made by every car, which they closely scrutinize to increase safety and dependability. There's an unstoppable disruption curve taking shape here, and I'll even go as far as to say that I don't think it'll be much longer before every major series highway in North America and Europe will be for self-driving cars only. Everyone who travels on these highways wants to feel safe, and knowing exactly how long it will take them to arrive at their destinations is a definite plus. Talk about a positive impact!

Blockchain Automation

Another unstoppable technological change involving automation will be the increased use of blockchain technology to generate "smart documents."

One of the long-term impacts of COVID-19 has been the forced closure of traditional office setting-type workplaces in favour of the ability to work remotely from anywhere. During the pandemic, companies had no choice but to realize that, provided their processes for communication and information flow were robust, they were able to operate successfully with fewer people. Going forward, this type of office automation will only accelerate as employees are not able to pass paper from one desk to another. Digitization isn't simply a convenient alternative anymore, as much as it's a firm workplace requirement. Companies won't go back to paper at this point.

This type of automation will have a similar impact on shipping and international freight. I'm proud to announce that in the near future at GCP, every part of the process, from the customer's order to the specifications for the factory to the shipping and customs details to delivery, will all be summarized within one "smart document" passed along the entire chain. It will greatly minimize the risk of human error, as will the potential for fraud.

Social Media

The final area I want to discuss is the evolution of social media. It's been said that money accentuates both the good and the bad in people. The same is true about social media. It can highlight the good news or blow the bad news out of proportion. It's absolutely critical for businesses to control their own narratives on social media today. If they don't, you can bet someone else would be delighted to do so.

At GCP, we take social media seriously. We want to be out there where people can find us and our products. Social media is and will continue to be an integral way to attract and retain customers.

Successful marketing attracts people to your brand and encourages them to get to know you, like you, and trust you. This process can take years. Being genuine and transparent in your interactions with customers will only fortify your relationships and set you apart from the competition. When we create content with social media, it's important to keep these considerations in mind. Using social media to establish your brand is like farming: We're planting seeds in cyberspace that will potentially yield a substantial harvest.

First Mover

With respect to technology, I'd like to share a few lessons I've learned over the years at GCP and Strategic Coach: Don't try to utilize or deploy technology on the cheap. Make sure there is a clear business need for any new technology. Make sure the technology is easy for the customer to use. Last but certainly not least, never be the first to buy an untested product. Make sure you're able to assess its practical impacts elsewhere first.

There's a short video I love on YouTube that speaks to the importance of the second-mover advantage. It's a short, three-minute video called *How to Start a Movement*. It opens with a person on a hillside on a sunny day. All of a sudden, he starts dancing like a crazy man. At first, all the people around him on the hill just either stare or ignore him. Then, one other person comes in and joins him in dancing like a lunatic. Once the second person gets involved, others gradually come along, one by one, until everyone around finally gets in on the dancing. The catalyst in this scenario is the second person, the individual I refer to as *the first mover*. This person is critical to the result because they represented everyone else in deciding they could be brave enough to take the leap and proved it was okay by actually *doing it*. People are always more inclined to follow the first mover more than they would the person who initiates the action.

First movers can also be looked upon as champions of your cause. These aren't just people who passively support you. These are people who truly believe in you and your ideas, and they take your ideas forward. Find these people, and keep them close. They'll have your back when it's time to take a critical step forward.

Even better, be one of these people yourself. Be the first person to follow. Be an optimist and a futurist, and see that technology can future-proof your business and make the world a better place, provided you've positioned yourself to harness its power.

-

CHAPTER THREE

How To Transform Fear Into Action

Fear is the brain's way of saying that there is something important for you to overcome.

—Rachel Huber

F ear is a major threat to a successful business. It can be paralyzing for entrepreneurs, executives, employees, and even entire businesses. There are several different versions of fear, among them the fear of technology, fear of the future, fear of the unknown, fear of failure, and even fear of success. Regardless of type, our fears can overwhelm us so drastically that they can be incapacitating both emotionally and physically.

But we dictate our measures of control over our fears. Many people reactively cope with the presence of their fear, but coping isn't a demonstration of control. It's only when we take the time to assess the root causes of our fears and why they exist and then create active strategies to overcome them that we're actually controlling our fears.

Any fear, regardless of type, exists only in our minds. It doesn't exist anywhere else. Fear is just an emotion. This quote from Sarah Baker Andrus illustrates my point:

If you take the word "fear" and make an acronym with its letters (F.E.A.R.), you can find a working definition of most of our fears: False Expectations Appearing Real. We expect a false outcome, and we imagine it so vividly that it appears real in our mind—so real that even our body reacts as though it is happening right now. Then, we usually take a course of action that makes us feel more comfortable, perhaps without even realizing we're moving in the wrong direction.

I'll contrast Andrus's F.E.A.R. definition with two related but opposite meanings:

Forget Everything And Run

Face Everything And Rise

The first is a recipe for disaster. The second is a recipe for success, one that business leaders need to embrace if they plan to succeed.

Whenever we experience fear, we need to rationalize our feelings of fear with facts. An effective response to feeling fear is to consider the immediate situation, broken down into components. What is the specific source of the fear? Is this fear justified?

I have a technique I find effective when dealing with feelings of fear. First, I isolate a single aspect of the problem. When selecting the aspect to isolate, I ensure it's something I can properly assess mentally. Then, I focus on it and bring about a solution to it in my mind. Even if it's the smallest assessment and solution, it's a beginning point. Once I resolve that aspect of the concern, I move through the remaining concerns using the same approach: face the concern, assess it, and negate it with a solution.

This is eliminating fear and F.E.A.R. with action. The idea is to reduce the fear mountain into separate little molehills, climbing and conquering each one until they no longer exist.

Allow me to provide you with an example from my own company.

In August 2018, U.S. President Donald Trump imposed thirty percent tariffs on goods made in China that were entering the United States. Not good; our products are made in China, and many of our customers are located in the United States.

At first, it appeared this would be a major crisis for our company. We had shipments on the oceans that would all of a sudden cost someone thirty percent more when they reached their destination. We estimated that we had approximately one week to come up with a solution.

I was very much afraid for the future of my business. I was thinking, *I've spent twenty years building this business. I'm in my mid-sixties. Is this how it ends?*

But it didn't. Why? Because I applied my fear methodology to the problem. I broke the large problem into smaller, more easily digestible problem aspects. Then, I developed a series of applicable measures to counter each aspect of the problem.

The tariff problem applied to my company. So, my first measure was to reduce my own salary by half, running a business case to determine how much of the increase could be absorbed by this measure. I next considered how the tariff problem applied to our production partners in China. After assessing all possible approaches, I concluded that convincing them to take a portion of the tariff hit as a short-term loss but a long-term gain that would result in the betterment of our business.

The final aspect of the tariff problem impacted our customers in the United States. By cutting our costs and lessening the impact of the tariff through our operations and that of our partners, we were able to pass on only a small fraction of the original tariff to our American customers. This was extremely helpful, as it allowed them to remain competitive in a commodity marketplace.

I carved the large problem into three smaller aspects of the problem and solved each one in kind. You know what? It worked. 2018 turned out to be our most successful year to date, and 2019 was even better. Not only did we face up to our fears, but we also effectively channeled them into creating solutioning strategies that would actually result in increased profits.

Now, this isn't to say that there's going to be an easy solution to every problem. However, I do believe the mechanism I just outlined represents an effective means to eliminate fear as a factor that can compound challenging problems.

Next, let's take a quick look at the fears that most businesspeople face.

Fear of the Unknown

We're all going to react to situations and certain things with feelings of fear; it's a natural inclination. However, there are ways we can neutralize these feelings so as not to let fear incapacitate us.

Take the example of people who work in hospital emergency rooms. These people are fully trained for almost any situation they may face. But every once in a while, they're confronted with something completely unexpected and often dangerous.

Imagine what would happen if these people had the first kind of F.E.A.R.—Forget Everything And Run. Chaos would ensue.

Instead, these people must have the mindset that when something unexpected happens, they follow a specific mental protocol: They clear their minds, get the facts, determine the best approaches, break down mountains into molehills, and develop and apply solutioning.

Similarly, in business, we have to ask ourselves: *What do we already know? What can we find out? What is the best solution?* By following this approach, we can at least create an assessment of the landscape that we can manipulate, eliminating any fear of the unknown.

Fear of Failure

When I started my first company, failure was not an option, although I didn't really think about it that way. I had given up a successful career, and my wife and I had one child with a second on the way.

I left my career as a top executive at a major firm to set up a company that would recycle tires using liquid nitrogen, a process that had never been unequivocally proven to be successful up to that point.

Failure would have been a huge problem for me and my family. And yet, this wasn't my biggest fear.

My biggest fear was that I was going to be stuck in a world where I would be doing the same thing year after year. Had I continued with my previous career path, I would have been very successful. But I would have been *bored*. I just couldn't see being in that world for any extended period of time. The fear of what I saw as my future was actually greater than my fear of failure.

So, I did what I had to do. I took the requisite steps to deal with my fear, and I overcame it. My second venture, GCP, has now been in business for over two decades.

Fear of Success

Fear of success is a lesser-known fear. However, for some entrepreneurs in particular, it can actually be equally as problematic as any other fear.

Many people may desire to be successful, but they really don't know what that truly means. They may have come from families with negative attitudes towards wealth and success. It's not uncommon for successful people to face some form of resentment. People sometimes perceive those with money in a negative light as being selfish and materialistic.

Consider the famous athletes and entertainers who don't know how to deal with success and the money and fame that come with it. A lot of these individuals, who we may imagine as being on top of the world, are not—they collapse into a world of excessive drug and alcohol use or even take their own lives after succumbing to the pressures of success. This is primarily because these people feel a sense of guilt when they look upon the fruits of their success. They wonder if they're truly worthy of their notoriety, the cars, houses, and everything else. These individuals don't see themselves in the same way we see them, and they wonder if they actually deserve any of it.

There's an old adage that I like to cite: *If you want to be rich and famous, try being rich first.* See how you like that for a while. Being famous poses an entirely different set of often-unanticipated problems, and very few people are able to successfully deal with both sets of problems at the same time. Unfortunately, many entrepreneurs haven't come to terms with the fact that it's okay for them to be successful. If you've put in the honest hard work that resulted in success, there's no need to feel guilty about being in such a position.

Fear and Your Employees

As a successful entrepreneur and business leader, you must also sometimes deal with the fears of the people who work for you.

At GCP, I'm very fortunate to have a good team. Leaders need to depend on their teams for advice and support and rely on them to oversee their own areas. There are a lot of situations that we can't get personally involved in. However, if you have good team members who can apply their own perspectives to problems, then you will get the information required to counter fear, both yours and theirs.

Be honest and direct with your employees. The more factual information they have about what's happening in your business, the more effective they'll be in controlling the inevitable fears they'll have. And that means the action they'll be required to take will be much more measured, informed, and confident.

My advice to leaders is not to be self-serving. Bring everybody along. I look at it the following way: If we win, it's because everyone on the team did their part. If we lose, it's because I made the wrong decisions. Or because I didn't deal with fear effectively.

Many business leaders are afraid their good employees will leave them. So, create situations and circumstances that make people want to stay! Some employees will leave regardless of what we do. This is something that will always be beyond our absolute control. But make it *hard* for them to leave. We have a much better chance of retaining good people when we demonstrate that we've placed our complete confidence and trust in them to take appropriate action when necessary and do the right thing. When employees feel as though we've adequately prepared them for their roles and invested significantly in setting them up for success, leaving becomes very difficult.

People will stay where they're wanted, respected, and made to feel secure. These things are worth so much more than money.

Face F.E.A.R.

As entrepreneurs and business leaders, we have to face fears on a regular basis. Remember that fear amounts to *False Expectations Appearing Real*. When we encounter a fear, we have two choices. We can *Forget Everything And Run*, or *Face Everything And Rise*. The second choice is so much better.

To deal with seemingly insurmountable fears, employ the mountain-into-molehills approach by assessing the concern that has provoked your feelings. Next, break this concern down into smaller aspects and deal with each in turn. Fear can certainly feel paralyzing, there's no question. But when we face up to fear and negate the potential for that paralysis to occur with action, we place ourselves in a position of control.

CHAPTER FOUR

Failure or Learning?

Those that fail to learn from history are doomed to repeat it.
—Sir Winston Churchill (paraphrasing George Santayana)

The path to success in business, as in life, is never a straight, unbroken line. We all suffer downturns, and we all suffer failures. What separates the winners from the losers is how we deal with failure.

Learning from our failures can unlock new possibilities in areas of creativity and innovation and can be catalytic in business success. Failing to learn is almost guaranteed to run your business into the ground.

To me, it's not important how many times you get knocked down—it's how many times you get back up again and continue the fight. When you fail, when you get knocked down, the most important thing is to learn *why* it happened and then take action to prevent it from happening again.

Let me give you an example of how learning from a colossal failure helped turn GCP Industrial Products into the successful business it is today.

GCP grew quickly over the course of its first three years. Then, in 2005, revenues dropped suddenly and sharply by forty to fifty percent. During this same time, the Canadian dollar plummeted.

We were hemorrhaging money. Some of the people who'd been with me from the very beginning resigned. Two of my largest customers left us to deal directly with factories in China. When I called my Chinese suppliers and asked what happened, they said, *"You stopped servicing them."*

That definitely knocked me down. But I got back up, and I resumed the fight. An important part of that fight was immediately learning what had caused this failure in my business and resolving it quickly.

Right away, I studied the details of the problem. I worked very hard to salvage the relationships with my suppliers, knowing that much of this had to be done in person. Eventually, I remedied the failure. And I learned from it.

Not long after that, my second-largest customer told us that GCP was difficult to do business with. In reality, what he really was that *I* was difficult to do business with.

I learned several very important lessons as a result of these twin failures back in 2005, and I've applied my learnings from both to the work we do at GCP to this day.

It occurred to me that these problems arose in large part because I didn't maintain close ties with the people who were critical to my business: my customers and my suppliers. I needed to take the time to understand what was happening in their worlds and what was important to them. I realized I had to try to look at the relationship from their perspective. What I needed to do on a continual basis was keep my finger on the pulse of the client—*every* client. Since then, I've followed the axiom:

"Eye on the prize and finger on the pulse."

I also learned that I was making that classic mistake entrepreneurs often make: I was trying to do everything myself. I was stretching myself too thin, in turn, not being able to give sufficient time and attention to aspects of the business that were really important.

This analysis led me to the decision that I needed to assign the right people to oversee four critical segments of the business: *logistics, customer service, sales,* and *quality control* (which included communications with the factories in China).

The people I hired in 2005 to look after these segments are all still with GCP today. Together, we survived the crisis. We learned from the failure. We rebuilt and grew a highly successful company. Having a specialized team around me allows us to thrive as a company.

Though on a much broader scale, Apple provides us with a related example of how to learn from mistakes and failures.

Apple has always been known as a company that creates products that people want. But, like GCP, they slipped up. Marketing and production weren't communicating. At one point, what Apple was selling and what it was actually offering was no longer the same thing. As a result, Apple terminated linchpin Steve Jobs.

The company continued to struggle following Jobs' dismissal. When he would eventually return to Apple, he had analyzed the company's mistakes and learned from its failures.

Apple's strength was always creating technology that people wanted to use. They have a streamlined number of products now, and Apple's focus is on what their customers want. Dell made the first MP3 player, but Apple made one that was better and easier for people to use.

———— ⊗ ————

When you fail in life or in business, how you react is your choice. You can take a negative approach. You can show anger and fear and cast blame on others. Or, you can choose to approach the situation from a more measured and methodical position, seeking ways to learn from the errors made to prevent them from occurring again.

Most entrepreneurs and business leaders don't make the effort to learn enough from their failures to enable themselves to adjust to a growth position. Take BlackBerry, for example. For many years, it was the absolute dominant force in the cell phone market. But it became too comfortable in its confidence that it couldn't be unseated. When the iPhone emerged onto the scene, BlackBerry's leaders didn't react. As Apple emphatically deposed BlackBerry in the marketplace, the company's executives took little action to assess the details of how this came to be in order to regain lost ground. BlackBerry's market share declined gradually, and its reign over the handheld device market ended in disaster.

Let's take a moment to quickly reinterpret the importance of examining the root causes of failure, learning from our mistakes, and converting a negative into a positive.

First of all, as I did in 2005, we often make the mistake of thinking we have to do it all ourselves. This is not the case. There will always be aspects of business we don't excel in, yet sometimes we take on these aspects anyway. We all have strengths, and we all have weaknesses. Sometimes, it can be considered a strength to recognize this fact and find someone whose skill sets complement your weaknesses by negating them.

When we fail, we have to be courageous enough to ask the hard questions. It doesn't matter whose fault it was if our intention is to determine the source of failure in order to remedy it and learn from it. When we remove egos and fear from the equation in favour of a desire to learn from failure so we can succeed, the ability to create and innovate are significantly bolstered.

Good generals know that wars are, in fact, the sum of a series of battles. When individual battles are lost, analysis takes place to determine the root causes for losses and draw up subsequent strategies with these analyses in mind.

This is how wars are won.

Chapter Five

Mutually Beneficial Long-Term Relationships

Business happens over years and years. Value is measured in the total upside of a business relationship, not by how much you squeezed out in any one deal.
—Mark Cuban, self-made billionaire and Shark Tank star

G CP is a multi-million dollar business, with our main production facilities located in China. This isn't unusual for a business in North America in 2023.

But twenty years ago, when I took my first trip to China, it seemed like a crazy idea.

I didn't speak the language. I didn't have a feel for the culture. I wasn't familiar with their system of government. I didn't have any experience with their business practices, nor did I have a sense of the ethics they applied in their business dealings.

I also didn't have any money to invest and didn't know much about the business that I was getting into. I had to ask my Chinese counterparts to bankroll the first deals, and audaciously, I had to ask them to change their operational methods to create a different product (which I'm now happy and grateful to say is the world-class product line we currently produce after our decades of working together).

Did I mention this all seemed like a crazy idea?

How and why did it all work out? It worked out because that first trip led to the creation of a mutually beneficial long-term relationship (MBLTR) with the people I would come to partner with in business.

My wife and I have been married for forty years. Has it always been easy? Of course not. Long-lasting personal relationships are never easy, and there are always challenges. But trust is one of the most important cornerstones of lasting relationships. If you're unable to establish a foundation of trust upon which to build your relationship, it will eventually collapse.

Respect is another key cornerstone. If you don't have respect for what your partner does and what they're capable of doing, and they feel the same way about you, the support you're able to offer each other will be minimal, if any support is possible at all. Divisions are gradually established, resentment presents itself, and the relationship ultimately ends.

Trust and respect have to be earned in a reciprocal measure. It's not enough that you have to trust and respect your partner. You also have to demonstrate, in turn, that you can be trusted and warrant respect as well.

Not always easy. However, establishing mutually beneficial long-term relationships is as critical to success in personal life as it is in business. In this regard, my first trip to China taught me an important lesson.

Before this trip, I had extensive business experience in Europe and North America, but I had been involved only peripherally in my dealings with China. My friends Roger and Phoebe Newman, who, at the time, had a company that was the third-largest North American importer of latex gloves from China, had pressed me for several years to do business overseas. For personal and business reasons, I had resisted. But I eventually changed my mind and agreed to take the leap, beginning with this trip.

As I was preparing for the trip, my friends informed me of a custom of the era: A businessperson's first trip to China was to be regarded as a "social visit" only.

I was shocked. I was going to travel halfway around the world, at my own expense, for a social visit?

Roger and Phoebe went on to say that the Chinese knew why I was coming, and if they wanted to talk business, they would. The worst thing to do would be to press them. *"Accept it for what it is,"* they said.

They were right.

And I'll tell you, it was one heck of a social visit. I drank with my Chinese hosts whenever they wanted. I ate whatever they put in front of me. I went where they wanted me to go. I saw what they wanted me to see.

My Chinese counterparts wanted to get to know me and then figure out whether they liked, respected, and trusted me enough to invest in developing a strong MBLTR.

This kind of relationship is now at the very heart of everything we do, and it's one of the key reasons GCP is a success. Business leaders should *never* overlook the value of a relationship for the sake of a quick transaction or simple financial gain.

I liken this idea to that of a building. First, you dig the hole by establishing your intention to develop something substantial. Next, you create a strong foundation by demonstrating genuine transparency and a willingness to be open, patient, and positive in your intentions to build relationships. The stronger and broader this foundation is, the more trust and respect you'll earn, and your building will be taller and so much more formidable over time. Creating these structures takes time, patience, and focus. And if you do your part to develop something worthwhile, the result can be special and long-lasting.

———◈———

The majority of our business consists of a small group of customers, many of whom have been with us for at least fifteen years. They've remained with us that long because they have confidence in us. One of the ways we build MBLTRs with our customers involves what I call The Risk-Free Supply Solution™. If a customer has a problem with the quality of a product we sell, we guarantee they will get their money back. No questions asked.

Now, clearly, I can't afford to give everyone their money back in the event of a big problem. We're simply not that big a company and don't have that kind of cash flow.

So, we have to have the kind of relationships with our production partners and quality control processes that afford us the opportunity to do everything we possibly can to provide a superior product before we deliver it. Our production partners understand that if we at GCP do our job flawlessly, it becomes their responsibility to pay for replacement products that fail to meet our customers' specifications. When we introduced this policy, I specifically recall being told: *"Other people are going to copy you. This isn't going to last."* That was in 2008, and no one else has done it since. And this is because they don't have the MBLTRs that we do with our partners.

The concept of MBLTRs clearly has to cascade through your company's employee population. Your employees have to believe in the idea, not only as it applies to your customers but also as it applies to your relationships with each other. Most of my key employees have been with GCP for more than fifteen years, and we all enjoy strong, secure relationships with each other.

Again, trust and respect are at the core of these relationships. A critical component in sustaining these relationships is ensuring that everyone has a voice and that they *feel* as though they have a voice. This demonstrates respect, trust, and a sense of importance and belonging that instills confidence in people along with a strong desire to succeed and give back.

As business leaders, one of your most important responsibilities is to first establish the framework that allows the opportunity for employees to succeed and then cultivate a workplace culture within that framework that empowers them to truly thrive.

Draw out the parameters of the playing field for your employees, coach them on how to play the game, and then let them play it. Be visible and communicative from the sidelines and join them on the field when they absolutely need it, but empowering them to perform more autonomously and achieve goals resulting from their own hard work is an amazingly rewarding concept.

I maintain consistent communication with my people. We have regular MOM (meeting of the minds) sessions with all the staff to give them an opportunity to share their perspectives from the front lines. I listen to what they think, how they're feeling, and what they might need help with. These people are the face and the future of my business, and they have a voice, not to mention a strong MBLTR.

In the early years, our Chinese business partners took me to places few foreigners had seen. As a result, we were able to access new business opportunities in terms of forging additional relationships with more partners and factories and discovering other businesses from whom we might be able to buy. I would never have found any of them without the strong relationships we developed with our initial partners.

Thinking back on those times, they felt like the Wild West to me. It's kind of a joke these days, but I literally wrote my first business plan for dealing with China on the back of a napkin in a hotel in Beijing. We were writing the rules and pulling it all together as we went. It was exciting, scary, and magical all at the same time. But my soon-to-be partners believed in me because I showed them they could. This was the basis for our relationships going forward.

My original Chinese partners still account for about fifty percent of our total business and are still our primary suppliers. I've visited more than 500 factories there, yet most of our business today comes from fewer than ten of them—and we have a solid long-term relationship with each one of them.

In the end, everyone was successful because of the strong long-term relationships we established on that first crazy trip so many years ago and the hard work we put in every day to create MBLTRs with suppliers, customers, and employees. It's not enough for the relationship to be beneficial to just one party. Every stakeholder involved has to be comfortable in understanding that our relationship is beneficial for them in the long term. Our relationships are, and we're all stronger for it.

After all these years, we haven't forgotten who brought us to the dance!

Chapter Six

Everything Starts With A Vision

If you are working on something exciting that you really care about, you don't have to be pushed. The vision pulls you.

—Steve Jobs

Having a vision of the future is critical for success in both our business and personal lives. Having vision positions you on a journey toward success. Without vision, you're never going to arrive at your destination, financial or personal, let alone be able to bring others along with you.

When people talk about vision, they tend to imagine grandiose targets: their own equivalent of the Taj Mahal. But my conception of vision is much more practical. The vision I'm defining here sets you on the path to your goal. It makes others want to follow you because you're instilling confidence in them that you know what you're doing.

If you don't have a long-term goal, there's a strong likelihood that you'll get caught up in what's happening now and lose sight of the bigger picture. And that's a path that leads to failure.

I believe everybody has the ability to create a vision for themselves. A reason many don't is likely because they don't grant themselves permission to think in that way. Maybe somebody in a position of authority once told them they couldn't. Or maybe they were told there was no purpose or point in it. By believing the naysayers, they resign themselves and their businesses to failure. To realize any endeavor-related success, a vision has to be formulated as a means to get there.

Speaking of the Taj Mahal, it's quite a beautiful picture. And it was once someone's vision. But the Taj Mahal had to be built one stone at a time. Right from the first moments this structure was envisioned, a process had to be devised wherein the initial vision was communicated, and then a forward momentum occurred toward the end result.

In business practice, if the communication of your vision doesn't include enough detail and specifics to allow anyone to action it, it's not a vision—it's just a pie-in-the-sky dream. A dream that could easily become a nightmare if your vision lacks a certain amount of development and refinement.

This quote from futurist and author Joel A. Barker perfectly illustrates my point:

"Vision without action is merely a dream. Action without vision just passes the time. Vision, with action, can change the world."

Mark Zuckerberg had a vision for Facebook. Bill Gates had one for Microsoft. And Jeff Bezos certainly had a vision for Amazon.

The success of these three companies is the result of vision, pure and simple.

When your vision is clear, it provides the motivation required to navigate the more difficult times and all the challenges that will arise. But vision should never be static; it evolves and changes shape as we make discoveries along the way. To meet challenges as they happen and to overcome them, vision must be adaptive while staying true to its core directives.

This has certainly been the key to GCP's success. When I made that first trip to China twenty years ago, I came away with a vision of the future. During this time, China was just breaking away from a fifty-year-long winter of tight Communist control. There were advantages and disadvantages involved, mostly centered around the fact that factories in China possessed superior technology but needed help from the outside to figure out how to manufacture world-class products. We were happy to help them, whereas many others were not.

I had initially thought it would be a ten-year commitment from which I could achieve some form of moderate financial success, with perhaps enough money to put aside for retirement. The reality is that it's turned out to be so much more than that. GCP is a multimillion-dollar business with many years of opportunity ahead, all made possible by a vision to use recycled rubber to create economical, environmentally friendly materials the industrial industry could use.

Of course, vision is critical in our personal lives, too. With respect to marriage, I had always had this vision that I never wanted to be married more than once. After my wife and I were married, while we were making our way as a married couple, we were uncertain how the relationship would continue to evolve. But we had a clear vision of what a successful marriage looked like, and we knew what we wanted our marriage to be.

My wife gets full credit for spending more than forty years with me, but she jokes it's really more like twenty years because I was away half of that time on business. She and I both say that she still has me on probation. But in all seriousness, this sort of kidding around underscores the fact that there are still expectations and responsibilities to be upheld. Your vision and relationships, whether personal or business-related, require consistent focus and must be nurtured if we expect them to grow and thrive.

⎯⎯◈⎯⎯

When the going gets tough and challenges seem insurmountable, giving up on our vision can seem like a relief. So many people do it, in business and life in general. But we can't. The rewards are too great. And I'm not just talking about financials. I'm talking about all the reasons for seeing a vision through to fruition, including the immense feeling of pride involved and that irreplaceable sense of accomplishment. The notion that you've made a difference in the world.

My vision has allowed me to achieve so much in the last twenty years. So, what's my vision for the next twenty?

On the personal side, I intend to live to be one hundred and ten years old. With our clients at Strategic Coach, some of the considerations we pose are as follows: *In the year before you're going to die, what would you be like if you could choose your physical situation?*

Your mental situation? How about your financial situation? And your relationships, and how you feel about yourself?

After they describe all those things, I then ask: *What's the actual likelihood that you're going to die a year later?*

There are health issues, and there are accidents and other scenarios that lead to a person's death. But people also often die from a lack of relationships, a lack of purpose, and lack of money. So, if you haven't run out of money, you haven't exhausted your purpose, and you've retained your friends and family and been fortunate enough not to have been faced with a fatal accident or illness . . . what's the likelihood you're going to live longer? After some consideration and visualization of the future, most people say they *are* going to live longer.

My original goal was to live longer than my father, who passed away at eight-three, so I extended my expectations to eighty-five. But now, my vision is one hundred and ten. This is a mindset. A mindset is how we perceive and consider the world around us and informs how we react to situations. Our mindsets and how we think are truly important. How we think determines what we do. In common terms, we can call people optimists or pessimists. The basis behind this rationale, why each person chooses to interpret the exact same situation in different ways, is attributed to their individual modes of perception and worldview.

A famous Henry Ford quote is particularly apt here:

"Whether you think you can, or you think you can't – you're right."

My goal to live to one hundred and ten means I have to have health, wealth, and relationships to sustain me for the second half of my life. Throughout, I commit to never stop learning, experimenting, and being excited about what's coming next, always engaging in my future.

My vision for the next twenty years in business is that of a world where artificial intelligence-based models can enlist computing power and algorithms to help bridge the great divide between supply and demand. The model would take into account what's influencing supply and demand in the world at any given time. Is there a disagreement between OPEC countries hiking the price of oil, which affects transport costs and the price of products? Does consumer unease over market reaction to a global pandemic historically decrease demand?

We should be able to gather whatever factors impact the marketplace at any given time and assess them using empirical data algorithms to predict future demand. This is the vision of my business future that I'm working toward.

⸻❖⸻

Vision is critical to success. A clear and compelling vision attracts the right people to your cause and progresses your momentum, even if you have no supporters early on. Your concise vision will propel you through to goal achievement. Everyone told me I would never make it with China. If I had listened to them, it would have been a self-fulfilling prophecy.

Don't listen. Shape your own vision, allow it to evolve accordingly, believe in it, and see it through. You *will* succeed.

CHAPTER SEVEN

Clarity Comes From Simplicity, Not Complexity

Simplicity is the most difficult thing to secure in this world. It is the last limit of experience and the last effort of genius.

—George Sand

You're driving at night, and it's so foggy you can't see the road. What should you do?

If you put on the high beams, all the light from them reflects off the complex web of fog into your eyes and creates confusion, making it difficult to know where to go.

But if you use your low beams or fog lights, which are directed down and to the sides of the car, they light up the centre line and the edge of the road. This simplifies the situation. You still may not be able to see too far ahead, but you can certainly see where you are and the way forward. Simplicity paves the way for action.

Deriving simplicity from complexity is a key component of success in life and business.

Complexity can reduce us into a state of paralysis. We have to be fully certain of what direction we're taking and why we're taking that direction. When we face complex situations, the confusion that often ensues can be emotionally taxing. This drain on our emotions can result in negative physical and mental impacts. When these struggles persist, and we're consumed by the moment, they leave little energy that would enable us to grow in any way.

When people deal with simplicity, they're happier. They have a clear direction. They have a bounce in their step and a twinkle in their eye because they're assured of what's happening around them and what they need to do.

In business, you need to see what's in front of you with clarity. When the way is clear, it imbues a simplicity across the landscape, making it easier to move forward and isolate and eliminate aspects that are not relevant to progression.

Many people do this by creating a "to-do" list of tasks they feel need to be done. I personally don't believe in long task lists because with more objectives comes additional layers of complexity.

I try never to have more than three things to accomplish in a single day. In this way, simplicity in task accomplishment bolsters confidence that these tasks can actually be done within a short timeframe. In a landscape uncluttered with multiple tasks, taking action is less stressful.

I call it my K.I.S.S. system. Most people know this acronym as "Keep It Simple, Stupid." Because I'd rather not use the word *stupid*, my acronym is "Keep It Sophisticatedly Simple." Leonardo da Vinci had a similar expression:

"Simplicity is the ultimate sophistication."

The idea of K.I.S.S. seems simple on the surface but is quite sophisticated on deeper levels.

For example, in late March 2020, during the first COVID-19 shutdown, we at GCP essentially had to close our company's office with twenty-four hours' notice. It was a huge task, but we made it happen. How did we do it?

The answer is that we were prepared with a solid crisis response plan. We readied ourselves for two years with the right tools and software and by considering the disasters that could happen. To be honest, at the time, I was thinking more along the lines of a snowstorm or a power outage, not a virus capable of killing almost seven million people.

Regardless, we had a plan so that there was little to no impact on our partners, customers, or staff when the shutdown happened. This was because we had already done the heavy lifting and set ourselves up for the best possible chance at success.

We adjusted quickly to the new reality. We had already purchased laptops for all our staff so they could work from home. Nearly all of them had preferred to come into the office, but as this was not possible, they at least had the necessary tools to do their jobs remotely. We substituted in-person meetings with online versions, using Zoom conference software and Google Hangout options.

In all, we handled the complexity of the shutdown in such a way that everybody could deal with it in a simplified, uncomplicated way. Simplicity on the surface, sophistication underneath.

Our experience in closing our office down within twenty-four hours is a prime example of why it's essential that business leaders convert complexity into simplicity in taking the most effective action.

Transforming complexity into simplicity can be difficult. The daily tidal wave of information coming at us is often more than the human brain can handle. When we filter that flood and focus on what we understand and are able to do ourselves, we can then seek out the appropriate stakeholders to take care of challenges that exist beyond our skill sets.

Take the task of investing money, for example. I don't invest on my own because I would be too emotional. I would paralyze myself with all of the information I would need to make an informed decision. This is why I have an adviser whom I trust to look after my investing. The needs of a business are vast. At GCP, we have lawyers, accountants, and people who possess the appropriate skill sets to reduce complexity as much as possible so that our way forward is as simple as it can be.

Gathering information is a necessity for a business leader, but it has to be done in such a way that complexity doesn't cause confusion. Filters have to be developed to eliminate needless peripheral information. Determine what's critical and what's not, considering only those things that are important enough to create an impact.

People generally fall into one of two categories. There are people who understand themselves and what's important to them, and there are people who don't.

People who are happy have figured out what's important to them: their relationships with other people in their lives and their relationships with money. Simple.

People who are unhappy and haven't yet figured out what's important for them as individuals may be doomed to live a life devoid of true happiness, and they'll have complexity to thank for it.

As humans, we all have the ability to make choices, rational or otherwise. Making good choices isn't always easy. But if we have big goals and ideals and want to live a life free of complexity, we need to recognize that simplification is essential when establishing the details surrounding these goals. There's a line I love in the Katy Perry song "Roar:"

"I stood for nothing, so I fell for everything."

It's so simple and so insightful. To stand for something means you have some semblance of how your future is going to play out. You designate the applicable filters in conducting an effective information-gathering exercise in relation to your goal and make decisions as you proceed. You bear down until you achieve your goal.

Here's one example of how I use filters.

Real Clear Politics is a website that gathers information from all over the place, from both sides of the political spectrum. It's an aggregator, and it's a simplifier. Like me, many people don't want to wade through the muck of information complexities on most websites, looking for the smaller nuggets of information relevant to them. But on *Real Clear Politics,* if I want to read about Korea or American technology, I just go to those subheadings. I enjoy the benefits of simplicity by having the option to separate and gather information important to me instead of fighting my way through a veritable quagmire of information I'm not interested in.

A phrase by Isodore Sharp from Four Seasons Hotel that I love to use summates another key method in achieving simplicity: *"Systemize the predictable to humanize the exceptional."*

When I think about recurring processes, I ask myself: *How do we set it up to work flawlessly without humans having to touch it?* Anytime a human touches something, there's an opportunity for corruption in the form of an error or mistake.

Computers, algorithms, and systems don't have relationships with people. As such, the more time we spend trying to reconcile mechanical problems that systems could deal with, the more time we are taking away from achieving things that only humans can achieve.

In essence, we're wasting the talents we have as human beings.

People still make the important decisions, even with all the machines we utilize today. My preferred approach is to try to provide people with the data they need to see the entire landscape and make informed decisions based on facts and trends. Otherwise, emotions would predict our decisions.

I always look for patterns and trends. If I happen to detect a pattern, I establish a process applicable to the pattern as a solution. This way, our emotional capacities remain available for effective human communication and interaction. When we become engrossed in tasks that prove too complex for us, we relinquish the ability to look after things that are simpler and necessary for us and our teams to complete.

We need to combine human capabilities with new technologies in using the tools available to us as a means of creating a more simplified world. This is the way forward.

Simplicity is your friend. Complexity is your enemy.

CHAPTER EIGHT
Crisis: React or Respond

A time of crisis is not just a time of anxiety and worry. It gives a chance, an opportunity, to choose well or to choose badly.

—Archbishop Desmond Tutu, anti-apartheid icon

COVID-19 was a prime example of how we cannot control what's going to happen in the world or what the winds of change may bring. But while it proved to be intensely debilitating, it was hardly unique. Over the past twenty years, business leaders around the world have been faced with similarly massive disruptions caused by 9/11, the global threat posed by the 2003 SARS pandemic, and the Great Recession of 2008, just to mention a few of the many crises that have stopped businesses in their tracks with little warning.

In any crisis, leaders need to compartmentalize the inevitable hyper-emotional response and do their best to mitigate rumors and speculation. Responding positively in the midst of a crisis is extremely difficult. Deferring blame to others and making finger-pointing excuses at obvious targets like the government is easy (and unfortunately popular). But this type of behaviour solves nothing. If anything, it breeds negativity, fear, and the potential for eruptions of violence.

Strong leaders sequester their fears, seek out the facts, arrive at decisions, communicate those to all stakeholders, and mobilize action plans against the crisis. Once again, the sailor can't control the winds but can certainly adjust his sails.

As a sailor, you can anticipate a change in the winds. You can see the ripples in the water beginning to move in a different direction. When this happens, you can't stay on the current course. You have to analyze the facts in real time and make decisions. Do I put the sails out, or do I pull them in? Where is the rudder best positioned? At what point will I need to fall back on the motor? And where are the potential areas that will force us to run aground? In sailing and in business, we know there are rocks in the water capable of destroying our vessel. Avoiding those rocks means keeping the ship afloat, completing our journey, and arriving at our desired destination.

In business, we avoid the rocks by carefully monitoring changes in wind activity in our industry. To do this, a leader must keep his thumb on the pulse of what's happening. It doesn't mean you have to be aware of every little detail, but it does mean being aware of what's trending, movement, and what's happening in the world.

The best way to do this is to start by making some basic decisions: What is the degree of severity of this crisis? Where do we stand in terms of impact and recovery? Based on that, what is the way forward in terms of what we can control today? How do we keep workflows going through weathering this crisis so that the return to normalcy is as brief as possible when the crisis has passed? Or is the crisis severe enough to warrant a change in direction?

In my experience, I've found this three-step approach works best:

1. *Step back and get the facts about what is happening.*

2. *Figure out what, if anything, you've actually lost.*

3. *Get the support required to formulate a go-forward action plan.*

When the novel coronavirus hit China, I could have easily thrown my hands up in despair and blamed others for the problem. But this reaction wouldn't help me effectively navigate the crisis. I knew COVID-19 would be a major problem for us. So, I took the time to educate myself. I researched the essential details of the virus: how it spread, the trajectory of the infection curve, and what countermeasures were working. I stayed informed on daily prognosis reports and acquired some very helpful information from a group associated with Peter Diamandis, founder and CEO of the X Prize Foundation.

All these information points allowed me to establish a basis from which I could make sound decisions, which, in turn, gave GCP the best chance of surviving a very uncertain business landscape.

In times of crisis, it's also important to cascade the information you've gleaned down through your leadership team and their verticals. In doing so, you're achieving two very important things: arming your team with worthwhile information and demonstrating that you've drawn up an effective plan, both of which will provide a level of comfort and confidence that will help them through the uncertainty. It's easy to lapse into a position of negativity in crises, and this approach will prove invaluable in avoiding such a tendency.

Communicate, communicate, communicate. Take great lengths to ensure everyone understands what's happening and what you need them to do. Talk to them in person. Show genuine empathy. Make lots of eye contact. Actively listen to them and hear their concerns. Make them feel wanted, appreciated, and valuable to the business.

GCP has a wide network of trusted sources in China and throughout North America. During COVID-19, we talked to them about what they were seeing on the ground in their areas. Knowing what they were going through on a daily and weekly basis helped us to ascertain the best possible ways we could support them.

I wrote a note to all of our Chinese partners saying, "*We're behind you. We support you. We're going to get orders in now. We're not leaving you.*" I did that because I anticipated their feelings of isolation. At that moment, there was a very tangible fear on their part that the world might not be coming back to buy from them ever again. It wasn't unreasonable to imagine that in their minds, they had been set adrift, cut off from the rest of the business world.

The responses I got blew me away. Our partners were so appreciative that we were still placing orders when no one else was.

I offered a very similar message to my team and our sales reps in North America. I wanted to know what they were experiencing, and they needed to be reassured by the fact that I was there to support them. It was critical to get a message of positivity across at that time. That potential lapse into negativity I mentioned earlier has to be one of the biggest considerations during a crisis. Negativity shuts people down mentally and emotionally and prevents them from looking ahead to the future with any sense of clarity. And clarity promotes confidence.

We assured our people—and through them, our customers—that our supply chain was secure. It was critical to get that message out; otherwise, our customers may have started to think: "*Maybe I should be buying from somebody else right now.*" We couldn't allow that to become a factor. In any crisis, it's critical to get the right message out quickly.

As a result of those conversations and with the support of my team, I felt that we could envision an end to the crisis. By mid-March 2020, even though it would still be early, given the eventual duration of the pandemic, I could feel that my company was solidly positioned to weather the storm. I felt we would survive because the fundamentals of our business remained intact. Our business was deemed essential, our customers were not closing down, factory production was, in fact, picking up, and people still needed the products we sold.

A final point to consider in dealing with a crisis is that it always provides an opportunity of some sort. I'm not talking about an opportunity at somebody else's expense; rather, my point is that the world is always just a little different every time we come out of a crisis. And how we look at the world changes, too.

The world's biggest crises and challenges can be seen as its biggest opportunities. Think about how the world eventually prospered in the wake of the crises I mentioned earlier at the start of this chapter: 9/11, SARS, and The Great Recession of 2008. Tangible opportunities will arise from COVID-19 as well.

Dan Sullivan, the founder of Strategic Coach®, says being an entrepreneur sometimes can be like being the guy who dives off the high cliffs in Acapulco. He has to jump when he sees only rocks below because he knows the next wave will bring the water back in by the time he completes his dive.

If he dives when there's water below, the wave will ebb while he's in the air, and the water will be gone by the time he intends to reach it. The difference between life and death is the knowledge of what will happen based on fact. In a crisis, an entrepreneur or leader must gather the facts and act swiftly to avoid the rocks that can potentially kill the business.

It's entirely likely the next twenty years will present us with more crises. No one knows what the next big calamity will be. But when it happens, business leaders can't just deploy cut-and-paste solutions from the past. Instead, they'll have no choice but to critically assess this new situation and determine a uniquely customized course of action based on their experience and the information that's available.

CHAPTER NINE

Protecting and Recharging Your Energy

Energy is the essence of life. Every day, you decide how you're going to use it by knowing what you want and what it takes to reach that goal and by maintaining focus.

—Oprah Winfrey

We've all heard the expression *"work hard, play hard."*

It's often applied to successful entrepreneurs and business leaders. But I've always seen this approach as being the wrong one. In fact, in my experience, it's led to failure, not success. The idea of expending my energy equally to my work and personal life actually disrupts the balance I personally need to be happy and effective.

Let me give you an example. I've been travelling across the USA and Asia regularly for nearly all of the last thirty years. My days and weeks would be jam-packed with loads of long flights, early mornings, and business dinners, followed by late nights. And I loved it! I derived so much energy from being 'on' as the center of attention. It was intoxicating.

I began to find getting back home and being back in the office challenging as a result. Life was not nearly as exciting in these spaces. In fact, I increasingly found it to be more and more of a drag. Upon returning from these trips, I didn't have any energy left to be a good husband, a good father, or even a boss. I would immediately start planning my next trip in an effort to recharge my energy levels.

I finally broke this cycle in the spring of 2019 after returning from what should have been a routine trip from Toronto to Boston. The delay details and frustrations aren't important. But what *is* important is the mood I was in. I was so exhausted and miserable that I was actually asked not to come into the office. At first, I was offended—this was my company, and no one was going to tell me when I could and could not be there. But then, I realized they were right. My behaviour was actually doing more harm than good.

The first decision I made in rectifying this situation was to give myself *freedom from travel*. Most people want to be free to travel. For me, it was the other way around. So, when the pandemic hit in March 2020, the travel bans actually worked in my favor; I had already had a year to prepare for being in one place for more than five days at a time.

A massive benefit I can attribute to this change is the significant increase in creativity I've enjoyed since I've chosen this new direction. I now have so much more time to think about important projects and take action with them. My relationships with my family have also improved. I'm around them more because I have more time to involve myself in their lives now. But more importantly, I'm truly "present" both mentally and physically—my energy levels and mood are right where they should be.

To me, the approach of *"work hard, play hard"* is really just a derivative of another popular expression: *"Burning the candle at both ends."* And that just doesn't work for me.

I believe success in business, as well as in life, is a marathon and not a sprint. To be successful in marathons, you have to be able to marshal your personal energy levels. You have to know when to expend it and understand that it exists in a finite capacity; effectively recharging that energy requires some thought. It's not as easy as stopping at an aid station for some water and catching your breath.

I've always believed that a means of recharging our energy can involve our passions. We derive a certain amount of real, legitimate energy from things we're passionate about—projects we work on, causes we involve ourselves in. The type of positive energy we generate in this context is a key to success.

Doing things we're not good at or don't like to do depletes our personal energies. Efforts that don't lead to positive results can drain our energy just as quickly. It's essential to protect our energy reserves; otherwise, we're not going to achieve the results we want in business or life. We're not machines. We're human beings.

Our energy must be directed. If left unchecked, it can be both a creative and destructive force. We all have the power to bring other people down, either with our words or actions. That same is true of the inverse: Others can usurp your energy and hurt you in the process.

In my life and business career, I've found that when someone is not happy with you, it can often be due to the fact that they're not completely happy with themselves. They lash out at you in a demonstration of projection because they don't have the courage or the requisite maturity levels to attempt to resolve their own problems.

It's very important to understand both sides of this equation in the interest of preserving your own longevity. Do your best to stay away from situations that could be considered destructive. Protect the relationships you truly value and cultivate them—put the work in to consistently fortify their strength. This is *worthwhile work* because we derive valuable, sustainable energy from these relationships. Conversely, avoid people who drown you in their negativity. Cut ties with those who've proven that they don't care about you. These people rob us of our energy, and they don't deserve it. They're best left behind as we pursue our successes in business and life.

Every one of us needs to understand how to recharge our own unique combination of what I see as four kinds of energy: *physical, emotional, mental,* and *spiritual.* The physical, mental, and emotional sides are highly interconnected. I believe we must be strong physically in order to be strong mentally and emotionally.

We don't function well when we're tired. If we're fatigued, we're not capable of making quality decisions or reacting effectively to situations. On the mental and emotional side, we're not going to make progress in achieving our goals if we're facing problems we can't resolve. For most people, the pain resulting from personal issues, such as marital woes or significant business concerns, depletes the vital energy we need to overcome these very problems.

I've faced business issues several times over the past twenty years, serious enough to have caused me a great deal of pain. It's incredibly difficult to overcome them without sapping your personal energy levels. But you have to find a way to do it—for your sake and for the sake of your company.

In an earlier chapter, I mentioned a method that's helped me. That method is to break down your problems into manageable pieces and then deal with them one by one. Make molehills of a mountain.

The last element I haven't mentioned yet, the spiritual element, is more complicated. I believe everyone derives some energy from the spiritual side, even if they don't care to admit it or maybe without even realizing it. Personally, I have a loose Christian faith. I'm not fanatical about it. I'm not a missionary or an evangelist. But the Bible is thousands of years old. It's a deep testament of emotional and spiritual truth. At times, I've used it to keep myself grounded.

There are always going to be people who say they don't believe in any god or in anything spiritual. But most of us operate on a set of principles. I believe we all need a moral compass, and we all need to place trust in others. Having had a spiritual grounding has allowed me to put faith in other people and other cultures, for that matter, whether in China, the United States, or here in Canada, where I live.

There's a concept I like called "emotional real estate." It's predicated on the belief that we all have a finite amount of energy. It's bound inside us. Understanding and protecting this idea fortifies this energy. We definitely need to be able to channel all of our personal energy to be successful.

Exercise your freedom of choice in focusing on what's critical to your personal success in business and life. Never, ever waste your precious, personal energy. Remember: It's a marathon, not a sprint.

Chapter Ten

Teams and Teamwork

Talent wins games, but teamwork and intelligence win championships.

—Michael Jordan

What made Scotty Bowman, the head coach of the Detroit Redwings from 1993 – 2002, achieve the record for the most wins in NHL history? From a strategic perspective, he completely understood the role of the coach as a leader, not as a star player. The coach's primary role is to have the right players on the ice at the right time, executing the plays they designed. The coach is responsible for strategy. The players are responsible for execution.

The coach has to have the ability to motivate each player to excel in their respective positions so that the overall success of the team can be possible. Goalies focus solely on goaltending, not playing centre. Defensemen don't play the wings. The skill sets are too different from one another. And beyond position, each player is a unique individual who reacts differently to motivational approaches. Everyone can't simply be painted with the same motivational brush. Understanding an individual's personality, perspectives, and motivations is critical in ensuring a coach gets the best possible performance out of everyone. When this is happening, and players are inspiring each other to raise their levels of play to higher standards, the synergistic strength of the team truly begins to take shape.

The ability to read situations and adapt approaches is also a key strength of coaches. Bowman was willing to evolve his style of leadership over the decades to align with an ever-changing National Hockey League. At the beginning of Bowman's tenure, it was not uncommon for coaches to use harsh, berating tactics in an attempt to bully good performances out of players. Toward the end of Bowman's era, changes to the league forced coaches to adopt a wider array of motivational approaches for players, some of whom were being paid exorbitant amounts of money and had adopted different attitudes towards their coaches.

When a hockey coach, or a coach of any sport for that matter, effectively motivates his team, championships are won. This is equally true for success in business. A well-selected, well-trained, well-motivated team can be unbeatable in the business world.

During football coach Vince Lombardi's tenure with the Green Bay Packers, a player on the arch-rival New York Giants once said after being defeated by the Packers yet another time: *"You could have given us Green Bay's playbook, and we still wouldn't have beaten them because they executed the plays so well."*

Championship sports teams know how to pull together under the coach's leadership. Similarly, a business can be successful only when its leader is a great coach who sets lofty but attainable goals, puts the right people in the right places, and then encourages them to put forth the best performance they possibly can.

As business leaders, we're responsible for telling our people what we want done, when we want it done, and why. After they've been sufficiently trained, it's not our responsibility to tell them how. The hockey coach doesn't score goals. He puts the best team in place to achieve that function.

During the past twenty years, my team and I have transformed GCP Industrial Products from a dream into a $20-million-a-year business. And we did this with only a small number of people. We succeed because each member of our small team is dedicated, committed, and motivated to achieve success.

Twenty million a year is what the team looks like today. But I had to build that team first; I had to put the right people in the right places. I had to train them and encourage them. I had to set broad goals for them and let them perform in their roles. As leaders, we would do well to keep what Richard Branson says in mind: *"I surround myself with people who have knowledge and talents in areas where I might not be so well versed."* Others use a similar axiom:

Surround yourself with people who are smarter than you.

———◈———

At GCP, my inner circle was built around four key objectives we need to achieve. Quite fortunately, I found the four people who are right for those roles, and they have been with GCP for more than fifteen years.

A successful business leader must demonstrate that he or she has a clear purpose and the right leadership skills to earn their trust. They must also have a willingness to be patient and invest in people. When a new person comes into GCP, I know it's going to take two years for them to become really effective at their job. Of course, I want to see progress every six months, but I recognize the importance of showing patience in having each employee take the necessary time to fully develop into their full potential.

Demonstrating patience and support grants us the potential to transform individuals who may have been mediocre in their roles in the past into highly valuable members of our team.

Never think of employees as a cost or a liability. Instead, think of them in the opposite way as valuable assets, investments in the future that appreciate over time.

———⦾———

It's obvious that people who are self-motivated will contribute immeasurably to our success as business leaders. As such, I tend to look at people as being either BIs or BNIs: *battery-included* or *battery-not-included*.

It can be difficult to motivate someone who doesn't want to be motivated, a classic trait of the BNIs. I estimate that to be successful, individuals need to be at least eighty percent self-motivated. These are the BIs. When this is the case, leaders can cover that extra twenty percent.

It's important to establish a clear distinction here between *managing* and *motivating*. Managing is providing individuals the opportunity to perform competently in a role through training and guidance, and motivating is quite different. When we're motivating individuals, we're working together with them to transform their competency into next-level performance.

The core ideas of what works well at a smaller company like GCP also apply to larger companies with many more employees. Regardless of company size, success hinges on cooperation and teamwork. There are a lot of systems out there for facilitating business communication and teamwork, such as Myers-Briggs and the DiSC assessment tool, which attribute success to achieving a greater understanding of an individual's primary motivators.

Both at GCP and in the work I do coaching entrepreneurs and business leaders, we use a system called *The Kolbe Theory*™. This system focuses on the cognitive aspects of your inherent drives and how they define how you take action.

Kolbe identifies people as belonging to one of four categories: *fact finder, follow-through, quick-start,* or *implementor*. Each category has its strengths and weaknesses. The following is a very rough sketch of the four categories.

The *fact-finder* likes detailed information and tries to simplify and clarify options.

The *follow-through* has an instinctive need to pattern, organize, and design.

The *quick-start* is the risk-taker who likes to drive change and innovation.

The *implementor* wants to build solutions.

Any successful team must have each of these categories represented. It's important to have people whose behaviours typify these categories to round out a balanced, robust team performance. Conversely, it's also important not to have too many people on a team with very high or low scores in the same category.

Really, though, it's ideal to have several people on a team who have scores in the middle range in all or most categories. These are the people who will ensure an even and necessary compromise. Today, this approach to building successful teams is critical, and I expect it will remain as such years and years from now.

The June 2016 edition of the *Harvard Business Review* featured a powerful article entitled "The Secrets of Great Teamwork." The main gist of the article was that teams in our current business world and those of the future are, and will be, quite different from the teams of the past. The authors identified these differences using the four Ds, saying they're far more *diverse, dispersed, digital,* and *dynamic.* This shouldn't necessarily come as any surprise to anyone in the business world, as we've seen these trends developing for many years.

Leaders will certainly need to understand how the four Ds impact their businesses, but the basic principles involved with building an effective team will remain the same, even as complexities in technology and business evolution continue to present themselves.

As I stipulated in an earlier chapter, business can grow only from simplicity, not complexity. We have the ability to create simplicity despite the perception that we're contributing to more complexity by building good teams because these teams are adequately equipped to handle complexity.

This is one of the reasons I believe the future is in the hands of people, not technology.

Over the next twenty years, status and titles will be less important, and people will be valued more for who they are and what they can do as specialists in key areas. The necessity to create strong new teams - to bring people together and to coach them properly - will be even greater. And this puts even *more* emphasis on ensuring the business leader, like a good coach, can effectively lead their teams by using inspiration and motivation.

Leaders themselves must consistently grow and develop if they expect to lead teams to continued successes. Leaders who fail to evolve in this way will not prosper. People, let alone leaders, who choose to grow and adapt to the ever-changing world around them rise to the tops of their fields, just as Scotty Bowman did. Those who choose not to embrace change in favour of relying on dated methods should pay heed to the fate of NHL coach Mike Babcock. He was brought in as a highly celebrated achiever who used old-school motivational methods, but those methods didn't resonate positively with modern young talent. He failed to recognize the consequences of the situation and adapt to alternative methods. As a result, he lost the respect of his team and, ultimately, his job as coach of the Toronto Maple Leafs.

If you want to succeed as a leader, see the consequences. Be a Bowman, not a Babcock.

CHAPTER ELEVEN

Belief

Never doubt your instinct.

—Anonymous

I've been a coach to entrepreneurs for twenty-five years, and I've learned that their perception of risk differs considerably from that of the average member of society.

When the subject of risk comes up during my workshops, I ask the individual a couple of questions. The first one is, "*Why did you start your business?*" The typical response is that they had a great idea or saw a gap in the market. Another popular answer is that they couldn't work within someone else's system.

Next, I ask, "*Did you think you would fail?*" The answer to this question is always a very affirmative *NO!*

My final question is, "*Did you take a risk?*" Silence usually follows this question. To this, I say, "*I don't think that entrepreneurs take a risk in their own minds. Other people see a risk, but not the entrepreneur.*"

Entrepreneurs have difficulty conceptualizing my last question because they always believe they'll succeed.

When I started GCP, I had been working at home for the eighteen months following my departure from my first business. I knew that I had to get into business again. I was forty-six years old with no savings or prospects for a pension, no income with teenage children, and college on the horizon. I felt that I had maybe twenty years left to make it so that my wife and I could have some form of "comfortable" retirement.

Getting a corporate job was not a viable option for me, having been on my own for ten years. Going back to work was simply *not going to work*. So, I did what I typically do.

I jumped.

In the same way that you would imagine jumping out of a plane without a parachute and figuring out how to land safely on the way down, I just completely went for it.

The first things I did were rent an office, hire a full-time assistant, and bought office furniture, computers, and a fax machine (high-tech back then!). Then, I took the family on a vacation. I said that I would figure it out when I got back.

But good things happen when you commit in this way.

When I returned from vacation, I got hired to be the President of a startup on a six-month contract. This would be all I needed to get going. The contract lasted seven months, and by then, I had my first order for a product from China to kick off the business that would become GCP.

I only gave myself one option, so it had to work. I had to *make* it work—I needed to be successful, so I believed I would. How it would actually work, I did not know, but I didn't worry about it. I believed that I could make it work.

The entrepreneur isn't afraid of taking risks. The entrepreneur is willing to jump, sometimes without a Plan A, a Plan B, or even a C. (A road sign that changes often once read, "If Plan A doesn't work, there are twenty-five more letters in the alphabet.") Entrepreneurs simply believe they must take risks to achieve their dreams. Interestingly, people who are not entrepreneurs may know what they need to do to start a business operation, but they don't have the belief necessary to take the risk and make the full commitment jump.

When we have that belief, powered by our dreams and raw ambition, it fuels the vision required to be successful as an entrepreneur. Our belief that we can succeed motivates us, energizes us, and propels us forward. It comes from deep inside us, and it's a powerful force. It provides us with the confidence we need to achieve what may be perceived as "impossible."

That confidence, powered by our belief, also helps us to push aside the negativity, the dire predictions, the objections, the obstacles, and any opposition that can often be offered up by those around us. Hesitation to consider any of these hindrances presented to us can trigger doubt, and doubt eradicates the confidence necessary for us to move forward with action. As the old adage goes:

"He who hesitates is lost."

All entrepreneurs have beliefs. Not all business leaders do. I've counselled many people in the business world over the course of my twenty years at Strategic Coach. At first, I thought I could teach people how to be an entrepreneur, but I was wrong. Entrepreneurialism is innate, and it can't be taught. I could teach leaders how to get to the edge of the cliff or the door of the plane, but their inclination to go ahead and jump comes from within.

The fear of jumping that most people experience—the uncertainty of outcome—doesn't exist in entrepreneurs. And if they do exist, they're so strongly eclipsed by belief that they may as well be nonexistent.

Albert Einstein is generally credited with the definition of insanity most of us are familiar with, the stuff of memes: doing the same thing over and over and expecting a different result. If we want a different result, we can't just fall into line with what everyone else is doing. Resilience, determination, and conviction allow us to blaze new trails. For the past twenty years, I've been told so many times: *"You can't work with the Chinese. They're not trustworthy. The first order is going to be great, and then the quality will continue to deteriorate until it's just trash."*

This sort of thing may happen when people neglect their working relationships in favour of "set it and forget it" operations. Having had a successful working relationship with the Chinese for more than twenty years now, I can attest to the fact that China certainly does not aspire toward that type of business relationship. Product quality and relationship quality work together symbiotically with my Chinese business partners in a mutually respectful capacity. The proclamations people make about inferior Chinese products and workmanship are patently false.

Having an open mind is so important. In time, I realized that people in China were indeed the same as everyone else. I demonstrated to them that they could trust me, and, in turn, they showed me I could trust them. We achieved mutual trust. Fundamentally, the Chinese operated much in the same way as citizens of other countries with whom I had worked in my previous career.

After I did my homework and found out for myself that there was significant potential in working with Chinese partners, my beliefs were affirmed. I never listened to the naysayers. I took the time to understand the Chinese people and their values and how they work. Yes, there are nuances involved when doing business with the Chinese.

On an early trip to China, an older, more experienced businessman told me that the Chinese won't be told what to do and that their response is much more favorable when interests are phrased as a suggestion. He was right, and our interactions were more effective as a result of this approach. Every time we met an obstacle and worked together to overcome it, my belief in the ultimate success of working with China became stronger.

The belief that entrepreneurs possess lends itself to a strong sense of self-reliance, a belief system that spans beyond simple self-confidence. Most business leaders are confident in themselves, but that self-confidence is limited to the parameters of their roles as business leaders. These individuals will sometimes sequester their inner beliefs in the interest of serving the requirements of their business roles. Entrepreneurs and their strong belief systems don't have limitations. They jump into their visions without parachutes and face risks head-on.

At Strategic Coach, I often run sessions for dozens of business leaders at a time. When they come in, I ask if people perceive them as confident outside that coaching room. They say yes. But then I ask them if they're confident inside the room. Many say no, or maybe.

Confidence ebbs and flows. But beliefs are carved in stone.

I enjoy dealing with individuals with very strong beliefs because I know what they will do. I know where they're coming from. As an entrepreneur, it's very important not only to have belief but to demonstrate that belief to others, particularly your employees. It's one thing to talk the talk, but the walking is what makes the real difference.

In a leadership capacity, you want to have people on your team who understand and share your core beliefs. When you effectively demonstrate that you believe in yourself and in the direction you're going, others will follow. And if you've got the right people, and they know what you're trying to do, you've got a team that can accomplish more collectively. Organizations where employees wait for marching orders experience consistent operational stalls, and most fail.

A successful business can be like a spider web. Each individual strand isn't strong on its own. But woven together with other strands, the nodes leverage each other's support and realize strength in interconnectivity. And when one strand breaks, the entire web falls open.

A final point: Belief must be positive. Strong beliefs based in negativity can be destructive.

Some business leaders believe they must win at all costs. These beliefs manifest themselves in arrogance, opposition, and a bullying stance, and they're myopic and destructive both for individuals and the companies they work with. I will not tolerate any of our customers or production partners acting in a way that berates or belittles my staff. All instances are addressed immediately.

I've threatened to stop doing business with several customers in this context, and approaching situations for this tack has prompted apologies from those who treated my staff poorly. Having a strong belief allows you to look after the individuals you've incorporated into your vision and look after them as you would yourself. This is a very powerful dynamic.

Never doubt your instincts. We all have instincts for a reason, and we're best served when we believe in them. Entrepreneurs learn how to evaluate and trust their instincts. It's similar to doing mathematics back in school. When we got something right, we filed it away in our brains. When we got something wrong, we asked ourselves, *How do I learn from that?* We can use this same methodology to develop our instincts.

CHAPTER TWELVE

Priority and Focus

The word "priority" was singular for five hundred years. What does "priorities" mean? Many, many "first things."

—Greg McKeown

Multitasking is a phenomenon that's often thought of as being essential to modern business. It's not. It's a myth, if not an impossibility.

Our society seems to believe that the more tasks you can handle simultaneously, the more effective you are. But let me ask you this: When we as a society refer to someone as a genius, in how many areas do we consider this person to possess this genius?

One.

It's surprising how the word *priority*, whose root is the Latin "prior" or "first," has morphed into something different over time. In the past, *priority* was singular. The Cambridge English Dictionary defines the word as *something more important than other things that needs to be done or dealt with first.*

Some *thing*. Not some *things*.

The idea of priority was thought of as being a singular notion from the time it came into general lexiconic usage in the 1400s until the 1900s when, illogically, the plural *priorities* was introduced into the English language.

Why is this lesson in etymology important? Because focusing on the single most important goal is the key to success. Multitasking sets us on the road to failure.

In my own life, there have been several times when I had multiple priorities rather than just a single priority. In those days, I never really settled on exactly what I was going to do. And this resulted in a lack of success in my life. I would do something for eight years, then immerse myself in a transition period, spending another eight years doing something else. I followed this same pattern two or three times. It wasn't a successful approach, and it didn't make me happy.

It was about twenty years ago that I realized that my problem was that I didn't stick with projects long enough to fully see them through. I didn't have a singular, focused priority in terms of what I was going to do with my business career or life. In the corporate world, where I had worked until that time, the thinking was that everyone moved on every two years because if people weren't doing that, they were stagnant and this observation negatively impacted one's chances of making it to the top. I realized at that point that I had to make some critical changes in my life, and that meant changing my entire outlook with respect to what it meant to be truly successful.

I was in my late forties during this period, so I figured I had about twenty years left to make the necessary change. If I waited any longer, I wouldn't have enough time to do it effectively.

As Zig Ziglar, American author and motivational speaker, once said:

"I don't care how much power, brilliance, or energy you have. If you don't harness it and focus on a specific target and hold it there, you're never going to accomplish as much as your ability warrants."

So, how did I come to fully commit the last twenty years to GCP? Two key considerations guided me toward this decision. The first one was personal. Both my father and my father-in-law had either chosen to retire just before they turned sixty-five or were forced to do so at that age. In their minds, they were perceived as being no longer useful to their employers. That's a terrible notion to consider on its own, on top of the fact that they no longer had complete control over their financial futures. This caused serious problems for them and their families.

I didn't want someone else to have that kind of power over me, and I still don't. I want complete control over all aspects of my future, particularly the financial ones. I'll decide when my time is up, not someone else.

The second consideration worked in tandem with the first. The only way I could have this type of control was to start my own company. I had been the president of a tire recycling company previously, and I remained very much committed to my personal need to do my part to protect the environment.

And that was it. I would make GCP my priority, my singular focus, because it allowed me to meet both of these goals. The way I saw it, having to rely on myself was less scary than the thought of someone else telling me what to do. Or even worse, having someone else occupy a position of financial control over my life.

Have there been problems? Of course, there have been. Will there be problems in the future? Certainly, and I'm ready to face them.

The need for entrepreneurs and business leaders to have a single priority will be even more important over the next twenty years as the world becomes increasingly more complex. But I do believe the opportunity for leaders to focus on just that one goal will become even greater. With the continued evolution of technology and the resulting trend toward specialization, being supported by others whose strengths are our weaknesses will become the norm.

For example, I'm aware that one of my strengths is developing projects. Following that initial development phase, I back away because I'm equally aware that execution is *not* one of my strengths. I put the right people in the right places; after defining the playing field for my staff, I watch them play the game from the sidelines, joining in periodically to lend my support and encouragement and help if and when needed. Every one of my team members, steadfastly supported by myself and my senior staff, believes in our single priority. It's essential to our success.

Let me give you an example of how this approach works in the game of hockey.

For decades, the Chicago Blackhawks were a National Hockey League doormat. They were moderately successful financially but a failure on the ice. When a new owner came in, he made it clear he had a different priority. Every game, when the Blackhawks hit the ice, he put a single message on the Jumbotron above them:

"One goal."

The team knew that the goal posted up there above them was to win the Stanley Cup. In the last ten years, the Hawks have won it three times. Contrast this with the Toronto Maple Leafs. They're a huge success financially, perhaps one of the wealthiest teams in all of pro sports, but they haven't won the Stanley Cup since 1967.

Why? Because their *goal* has to be to win the Cup. But oddly enough, it's never been the singular priority. Neither the owners, the team management, nor the players are truly committed. They all know the money will continue to flow in and that the tried-and-true fan base will never leave them, regardless of the team's ongoing failure to win.

At GCP, our focus is making it easy for people to do business with us. Our core purpose is to help people and organizations grow. As GCP's leader, I run everything through that filter. If I'm not helping my team, customers, and partners grow, I'm not accomplishing the singular priority I've made myself responsible for.

Good leaders recognize that they must always maintain a singular focus. Being a "Jack of All Trades" only means we're a master of none. Throwing approaches against the wall over and over again to see what sticks is just spinning our wheels, not gaining any traction and ultimately leading to failure. Yet, a lot of entrepreneurs still follow this formula.

Leaders have to remember that even as the world gets more complicated over the next twenty years, priority is a singular notion. Have one, and follow it to success.

.

CHAPTER THIRTEEN

Never Waste a Crisis

You never want a serious crisis to go to waste. Why? Because it's an opportunity to do things you could not do before.

—Rahm Emanuel

My wife and I were caught in Hurricane Emily in Bermuda in 1987. We had an eyewitness view of the destruction, and it was absolutely devastating. Crisis situations resulting from natural disasters are catastrophic emotionally and economically and require a massive recovery effort.

COVID-19 packed a similarly devastating punch that wreaked emotional and economic chaos on a far greater scale. It's the worst such crisis to impact human civilization since the Second World War.

Islands and cities battered by hurricanes and other natural disasters eventually recover. Oftentimes, they can grow even stronger in the bargain. With respect to COVID-19 and its catastrophic impact on most businesses, we press on. Even if a business doesn't make a complete recovery in its current form, forward-thinking on the part of its leaders allows it to transmute into something else. Something stronger.

A hurricane's devastation is swift and intense but relatively short in duration. The impacts of the pandemic, as we emerge from its clutches, will be long-lasting and far more devastating over time. But every cloud has a silver lining, and that silver lining is the opportunity for business leaders to build back stronger.

The following two modes of thinking can help entrepreneurs and business leaders not only survive through crises but, in fact, thrive through them. The first is what I call the three phases of human perspective during a crisis:

1. *Reaction and fear (negative)*

2. *Clean up the mess (negative with positive)*

3. *Find a way to move forward (positive)*

The second is the three types of W.I.N., a concept created by Jeff MacInnis, Corporate Explorer and WIN Thinking Director.

1. *What's Important Now?*

2. *What's Important Next?*

3. *What's Important Never?*

I argue that the third one, *never*, is the one most crucial to moving forward. I offer that advice based on the fact that GCP has weathered many crises over its twenty-plus years of existence, including 9/11, SARS, the Great Recession in 2008, a port strike in Los Angeles, and the 2008 Beijing Olympics when they banned all trucks from the roads in the city (which, incidentally, also blocked shipments of goods that my company and others required to maintain standard operations).

In each of these crises, our business halted temporarily, just as it did in the early stages of the COVID-19 pandemic. And in all cases, we not only survived; we emerged to thrive. And as we move through the final phases of COVID, I know that GCP will continue to thrive because we know exactly what to do.

GCP is in the business of physically transporting goods internationally. I believe people will always need the commodities we sell in some capacity. When you find yourself in the midst of a crisis as a business leader, it's important to use the opportunity to reconceptualize process optimization in new and more effective ways beyond simply rebuilding what was lost. By missing the chance to build back better, we're leaving ourselves open to the possibility of being overtaken by our competitors.

Many theorists and popular leaders—from Niccolò Machiavelli to Winston Churchill to Rahm Emanuel—have echoed the general sentiment: *Never waste the opportunity offered by a good crisis.*

Let's apply the rationale using the two frameworks I mentioned earlier.

Reaction: Initially, we tend to panic because we don't know exactly what will happen next. This gives way to fear, which can have a paralyzing effect. To counteract fear, I close down a little and look at what I've got to do immediately. I go into survival mode, doing what I need to do to ensure my business survives to fight another day.

Cleanup: After the initial reaction, I start tackling the short-to-medium term problems. As you'll recall from earlier chapters, I make molehills out of the mountain. I break problems down into manageable chunks, tackling them individually until I can see the path forward.

Move forward: This is the critical phase. As a business leader, I determine not only how to survive the crisis but how to rebuild. How to *thrive.*

Where the W.I.N. system is concerned, it really helps leaders manage crises effectively by focusing on what's urgent and important at the moment and what's not urgent and not important.

What's Important Now? Ask yourself these questions: What are all the things I must do *right now?* What's the most important thing I must do *right now?*

What's Important Next? After you've answered that first question—and taken the time to deal with it—start looking a little further forward to prepare for what's ahead. In the case of my company, I always need to be aware of what's happening with the United States government and its relations with China. To prepare for what's ahead, I have to communicate with my suppliers, who are in China. I also need to speak with my clients in the United States. How, if at all, do they see the future changing?

What's Important Never? This is the step I think is the most important. Ask yourself what you can stop doing at this point in the crisis to focus on top priorities for the future. You may be surprised by the answer. But it's crucial to ask yourself this question and land on an honest answer. Otherwise, you're simply rebuilding the past and not planning for the future.

My son Craig, Marketing Vice-President at GCP, participated in a webinar recently about how COVID-19 is initiating changes we thought wouldn't happen for another twenty or thirty years.

My son-in-law is an engineer. He was approached recently by a company that makes robotics products. Normally, they get about fifty orders per year, but as people began to see how the world was changing as a result of the pandemic, the company suddenly had a backlog of more than two hundred orders(!).

In many ways, the crisis brought about by COVID-19—and the opportunities it will create for the future—is reminiscent of the devastation of the Second World War. In addition to the horrific human cost and the geopolitical consequences, the Second World War destroyed the world's international trade infrastructure. All the pre-war supply lines were either wiped out or radically changed, with most of the factories around the world being repurposed for the mass production of war munitions. All of these changes had to be reversed or reconfigured following the end of the war to accommodate a new postwar world. And the economic toll was devastating.

Tomorrow's world of business will be significantly different with the rise of digitization. Crises will continue to loom, however, just in different forms. Cyberattacks are already paralyzing the world's most powerful, seemingly impenetrable organizations.

Preparation is perhaps the most important line of defense where crises are concerned, and as leaders, we need to have drawn up highly detailed and actionable solutioning scenarios so as not to be reactive but *proactive*.

Reactivity means we likely just get through the crisis more or less unscathed. But proactivity gives us an opportunity to actually *thrive* in the face of a crisis. And, as the old saying quoted at the beginning of this chapter goes, maybe even achieve things we were unable to achieve before the crisis presented itself.

We never want to waste a chance to do that.

CHAPTER FOURTEEN
Time

Time is clearly the most precious resource we all have.
—Steve Jobs

Time is the great equalizer. Elon Musk, Richard Branson, you and me . . . we all submit to time. No one can expand the amount of time in a day, a week, a month, a year, or a decade. The big differentiator that determines whether we are happy or not, whether we succeed or not, is what we do with the time we have.

I believe two factors make a big difference for everyone: finding work that makes us happy and productive and thinking of time as an investment, not an expense.

In finding the work that gives us satisfaction, we have to afford ourselves the liberty of experimentation. We explore a variety of areas to eventually find work that doesn't necessarily feel like work at all. Marketing guru Joe Polish puts it this way: *We can do things that are "work," or we can do things that are E.L.F.---easy, lucrative, and fun.*

Polish, the founder of Genius Network and GeniusX, argues that three types of entrepreneurs exist. Most of them have a H. A.L.F. Business™—Hard, Annoying, Lame, and Frustrating. A successful person may actually have a Hard, Annoying, LUCRATIVE, and Frustrating business, but it's still H.A.L.F. The third type of entrepreneur, the truly successful one, has an E.L.F. Business™. Because if it's easy for us, we're probably good at it. And if we're good at something, there's very little stress involved in doing the work and plenty of opportunity for success. If we're having fun, we're enjoying what we do, and that joy is contagious to those around us.

Thinking of time as an investment can make all the difference in the world. Stephen Covey, the author who popularized the "time management matrix," expresses it this way:

"The key is in not spending time, but in investing it."

We can pass our time doing useless things or useful things. When we're busying ourselves with useless tasks, we're spending time. Investing time in useful things is different. An investment creates returns in the future that provide a personal or business benefit. An expense, on the other hand, is gone the minute it's paid.

We may have to invest a great deal of time to achieve the results we want. For example, I've been coaching other business leaders for twenty-four years. At first, it wasn't so easy for me. And I really wasn't very good at it, either. But I enjoyed the coaching a lot, so I invested time and effort to improve myself. In his bestselling book *Outliers*, author Malcolm Gladwell popularized the theory that if we spend 10,000 hours practicing a particular skill, we will indeed achieve mastery over that skill.

And he's right. Almost twenty-five years after I began coaching, I can tell you I'm a lot better at it, and I can certainly appreciate how the investment of 10,000 hours of practice time makes me a better coach.

If we spend our time in activities that we're not good at and don't really like, we don't really get any better. This isn't an investment; it's a waste. The key is to assess where best to invest our time so as to generate the greatest returns. Oftentimes, the most common mistake that business leaders make is to assume they can or should do everything without considering the required expenditure of time, whether or not they can perform a wide scope of tasks with the prerequisite level of skill for each, and whether this effort will produce the desired results.

It's key for business leaders is to recognize where the members of our teams should be passing their time. Because if they're not doing that, they're not investing it. They're wasting it—and in turn, so are we.

Assume a business costs $1,000 an hour to run. By this rationale, it costs $1,000 for every wasted hour. Every hour that isn't used productively costs another $1,000. In this way, we're holding a fresh $1,000 bill in one hand, striking a match, and holding the flame to that bill with the other hand every hour.

It starts at the leadership level. Business leaders have to be mindful of their vulnerabilities, areas to which their strengths and individual skill sets don't apply. A vulnerability shouldn't be considered a weakness, however - when vulnerability is recognized and accounted for, this mindfulness can actually be considered a strength.

I believe that human beings genuinely want to help others. If we as leaders are being open and honest, and we're forthright with regards to our shortcomings in certain areas, I think most people would be happy to help us out.

No one wants to help the assholes. But even with difficult segments of people, when a positive, honest approach is used to assess what isn't working, it's effective. When the leader asks, *"How can we make it work?"* and demonstrates a genuine interest in working together to remedy the problem, it's hard not to open up.

A valuable investment of time is in *relationships*. We have more control over these investments than any other financial investment we may make. In our personal lives, we get to choose who we spend time with and what we do with these people. Managed wisely, the time we pass cultivating relationships will be some of the best investments we can make.

Remember, time is neither created nor destroyed. Once it passes, it's gone forever. We don't ever get it back. We can extend our time by being involved in the things we love to do, by looking after ourselves, and by making sure that we invest our time in the work we love and the people we want to share it with. As the ancient Greek philosopher Theophrastus once said: *"Time is the most valuable thing a man can spend."*

Afterword

As I've mentioned, before 2020, my company had several "disaster plans" worked out for the types of emergencies one would normally expect. However, like most people around the world, I certainly did not expect a pandemic of such massive consequence to emerge and wreak the havoc it would.

Even though we now see the other side of COVID-19, it'll still be several years before we fully achieve a "new normal." The world will never be the same as it was before 2020.

Remote work is here to stay. There's been a return to the office in some business segments, but increasing numbers of people will work from home in the future.

And the pace of technological change is skyrocketing. As such, we as business leaders must now fully embrace digitization. Before 2020, so many processes were carried out physically. Those days are ending quickly.

Fortunately for us at GCP, even before COVID-19, our customers, production partners, and sales reps rarely came into our office. My staff all have the proper equipment to work from home. A few, including myself, still occasionally come into the office for specific purposes. But we'll never go back to the days when we all worked in one great big company headquarters-type space.

We always had one foot in the future and one foot in the past. Now, we've got everything but our big toe in the future at GCP. As a futurist and an experienced international businessperson, I know the world will bounce back and businesses will thrive again.

As a business leader, I still wholeheartedly believe in a brighter future. I still believe in the ingenuity and the capability of the men and women of the human race and the resilience of well-intentioned human nature.

Leaders everywhere, of any description, are best served doing what they can to foster cooperation for everybody's benefit. I've got grandchildren, and I see a bright future for them and my children, who are still thirty years younger than me.

Don't ever lose hope. Continue to work and fight for what you feel is just. If we all look after ourselves and the people around us, the world will turn out just fine.

I genuinely believe that. I feel like there were benefits associated with the pandemic, and one of those benefits was that people will trust each other more, even if they trust institutions and governments less. In the future, it'll be even more important to focus on the immeasurable value of relationships. Institutions will have to adapt in order to avoid becoming irrelevant in ordinary life.

As it is for institutions, the most significant risk for businesses is assuming the world will return to the way of life we experienced before the pandemic. Big mistake. The world never quite goes back to the way it was before a major disruption. Think about air travel prior to September 11, 2001.

The people who work for you have different mindsets than they did in 2020. They see things in a different way now. We all do. And none of us are going back. Not our customers, not our stakeholders, not our family nor friends.

We have no choice but to recognize this and adapt. Adaptation enables us to get ahead of the shift and positions us to take advantage of it.

As I look forward to the next twenty years, I truly believe that failure to learn from the lessons of the past will result in continued failure going forward.

Learn. Adapt. Evolve. These are the unequivocal keys to success in business and in life.

"Eye on the prize, and finger on the pulse."

Acknowledgments

A book to go from an idea to a fully written and published book is a collaboration of many people, all with unique and complementary talents. *Nimble Future* is a product of this type of collaboration.

My heartfelt thanks go to my writing partners, Christopher Shulgan and Jim Shepard at Ghost Bureau, whose countless hours helped bring my thoughts and ideas to the printed page. Also, to Brent Jensen of Storyphoria, whose unique ability to craft words into my voice made *Nimble Future* ready to publish.

Without my amazing team at GCP Industrial Products, I would not have had the time or experiences to contribute to *Nimble Future*. Also, my appreciation goes out to Dan Sullivan and Babs Smith, the founders of Strategic Coach®, who saw something in me and gave me the opportunity to coach entrepreneurs. This book would not have happened without the experiences and encouragement from my team and the Coach community.

Kary Oberbrunner, Travis White, and the team at Igniting Souls Publishing were able to transform a personal manuscript into a full-fledged book worthy of publishing. *Nimble Future* is truly a result of our collaboration.

Last but certainly not least, my sincere appreciation and gratitude goes to my wife, Karen, and my adult children, Craig and Kristy. These three people have been my rock and safe place that I have been able to rely on and come home to for more than 40 years. This stability in my life has allowed me to see the world and look forward to the future without having to be concerned about my past or present.

About The Author

Gary Mottershead is always looking toward the future.

With over 30 years of experience working with recycled rubber and industrial products, Gary is leading his industry to new ways of doing business with manufacturing partners around the globe. Not only has he managed to mitigate the risk from using international sources, but he's also shifted these imports from being perceived as "bargain goods" to being proven as reliable, quality materials used in critical applications.

With a background in manufacturing and chemical engineering, Gary ventured into entrepreneurship in his mid-30s by pioneering cryogenic tire recycling with the establishment of Recovery Technologies Inc. This marked the beginning of Gary's entrepreneurial journey, eventually leading him to Strategic Coach®, an organization committed to mentoring entrepreneurs. Shortly thereafter, Gary transitioned into a coaching role himself, continuing to guide entrepreneurs globally for over 25 years. His current company, GCP Industrial Products, is the leading vendor of Industrial sheet rubber (made from recycled rubber) in North America.

Residing in Waterloo, Ontario, Canada, Gary shares his life with his wife, Karen. They are proud parents of two married children and loving grandparents to two grandchildren. Gary is also the author of *Guanxi: The China You Never Read About* and *The Right-Shoring Advantage*. Additionally, he hosts a bi-weekly podcast titled *Clarity Generates Confidence*, offering insights and inspiration to his listeners.

Whether he's coaching, writing, or podcasting, by asking questions about what's most important, Gary helps create a motivating picture of the future and a plan for transcending your past.

Endnotes

1. *Simon Sinek, "Start with Why – How Great Leaders Inspire Action: Simon Sinek: Tedxpugetsound," YouTube, September 29, 2009, https://youtu.be/u4ZoJKF_VuA?s i=K6p4HPF3nDIJbXus.*

Clarity Generates Confidence™ Podcast
with Gary Mottershead

Get ready for a series filled with insightful conversations, inspiring narratives, and actionable advice to boost your personal and professional growth.

GCPIndustrial.com/Podcasts

THIS BOOK IS PROTECTED INTELLECTUAL PROPERTY

EASY IP™

The author of this book values Intellectual Property. The book you just read is protected by Easy IP™, a proprietary process, which integrates blockchain technology giving Intellectual Property "Global Protection." By creating a "Time-Stamped" smart contract that can never be tampered with or changed, we establish "First Use" that tracks back to the author.

Easy IP™ functions much like a Pre-Patent™ since it provides an immutable "First Use" of the Intellectual Property. This is achieved through our proprietary process of leveraging blockchain technology and smart contracts. As a result, proving "First Use" is simple through a global and verifiable smart contract. By protecting intellectual property with blockchain technology and smart contracts, we establish a "First to File" event.

Powered By Easy IP™

LEARN MORE AT EASYIP.TODAY